Memorize the Faith!

(and Most Anything Else)

Kevin Vost, Psy.D.

Memorize the Faith!

(and Most Anything Else)

Using the Methods of the Great Catholic Medieval Memory Masters

SOPHIA INSTITUTE PRESS®
Manchester, New Hampshire

Printed in the United States of America

Cover art and illustrations by Ted Schluenderfritz

Biblical citations are taken from the Revised Standard Version of the Bible (© 1971 by Division of Christian Education of the National Council of the Churches of Christ in the United States of America), unless otherwise noted.

Sophia Institute Press®
Box 5284, Manchester, NH 03108
1-800-888-9344
www.sophiainstitute.com

Library of Congress Cataloging-in-Publication Data

Vost, Kevin.
Memorize the faith! (and most anything else) : using the methods of the great Catholic medieval memory masters / Kevin Vost.
p. cm.
Includes bibliographical references.
ISBN-13: 978-1-933184-17-3 (ISBN-10: 1-933184-17-5) (pbk. : alk. paper) 1. Catholic Church — Study and teaching. 2. Catholic Church —Doctrines. 3. Memory. 4. Mnemonics. I. Title.

BX895.V67 2006
282.071 — dc22

2006001905

06 07 08 09 10 9 8 7 6 5 4 3 2 1

To
Marjorie Margaret (Leahy) Vost
(1925-1999):
she bore the fruits of
gentleness and kindness

and to
James Henry Vost
(1926-2005),
my pillar of strength and fortitude

Contents

Notes to Readers of This Book

A Note to Adult Readers xiii

A Note to Younger Readers xvi

A Note to Homeschoolers xx

Memory Master Tips and Facts. xx

Part 1

The Stone the Builders Rejected

1. How to Use This Book 5
2. The Memory System of St. Thomas Aquinas 21

Part 2

As for Me and My House

3. The Ten Commandments 31
4. The Seven Capital Sins 35
5 The Seven Virtues 43
6. The Nine Beatitudes 49
7. The Seven Sacraments. 55
8. The Twenty Mysteries of the Rosary 61

Part 3
In My Father's House Are Many Mansions

9. The Four Marks of the Church 75

10. The Four Last Things. 81

11. The Five Precepts of the Church. 85

12. The Six Sins Against the Holy Spirit 89

13. The Seven Gifts of the Holy Spirit 95

14. The Seven Spiritual Works of Mercy 101

15. The Seven Corporal Works of Mercy 105

16. Ten Holy Days of Obligation in the Latin Rite of the Catholic Church 111

17. The Twelve Apostles 117

18. The Twelve Fruits of the Holy Spirit. 121

19. The Fourteen Stations of the Cross. 125

Part 4
Grow in Grace and in Knowledge of Our Lord

20. Five Proofs of the Existence of God 131

21. The Forty-Six Books of the Old Testament. 137

22. The Twenty-Seven Books of the New Testament 157

23. Twenty-One Centuries of Church History 171

24. The Twenty-Five Parts of the Cardinal Virtues . . . 185

25. The Forty-Four Daughters of the Capital Sins 193

26. Three More Mnemonic Systems 199

27. Twelve Red-Letter Sayings of Jesus Christ 211

Part 5

Remember What I Preach

28. Applications for All Ages 221

29. How to Teach This System to Your Children 229

Conclusion: From Memory and
Understanding to Faith and Works. 241

Afterword: An Ode to Memorization 247

Biographical Note: Kevin Vost 249

Acknowledgments

To the many friends, colleagues, and teachers who have contributed either directly or indirectly to the creation of this book, I say thank you, for what you have taught me and for the encouragement you have provided. Although you might not be named, you are remembered (as I hope to show you when I sign your copy).

And now, for a few names.

The Dominican sisters and Viatorian priests of Springfield, Illinois, taught me respect for the intellect in my youth. Dr. Karen Kirkendall of the University of Illinois at Springfield guided my master's level work on memory and opened for me the door to university teaching. A generous mentor, she instilled in me a deep respect for developmental and cognitive psychology. Dr. Ronald F. Zec of the Southern Illinois University School of Medicine guided my doctoral work and modeled unmatched passion for the neuropsychology of memory and aging. He is truly a modern master of memory. Mr. Todd Aglialoro and Dr. John Barger of Sophia Institute did so much to shape what is good in this book that I could write a book about it. The imperfections were generated from my own keyboard.

Last, but never least, I must thank Kathy, Eric, and Kyle Vost for their forbearance as I clicked away at these keys and talked so much of memory. They give me my best memories.

Notes to Readers of This Book

"When I was a child, I spoke like a child,
I thought like a child, I reasoned like a child:
when I became a man, I gave up childish ways."

1 Corinthians 13:11

A NOTE TO ADULT READERS

Do you see memorization as one of those childish things you have gladly given up? Perhaps you have some less-than-pleasant memories of having to memorize things in childhood. Did you have to remember the books of the Bible in a Sunday-school program, or the fifty state capitals in fourth-grade geography? Wasn't it boring?

Perhaps you were taught a few mnemonic (memory aiding) tricks along the way — HOMES for the Great Lakes (Huron, Ontario, Michigan, Erie, Superior), or "Every Good Boy Does Fine" (EGBDF) for the lines of the treble clef. Maybe you even picked up "My Very Eccentric Mother Just Served Us Nine Pizzas" or "Man Very Early Made Jars Stand Up Nearly Perpendicular" (MVEMJSUNP) to help you remember the nine planets in their order from the sun (Mercury, Venus, Earth, Mars, Jupiter, Saturn, Uranus, Neptune, Pluto). But I'll bet it was still more drudgery than fun, right?

And you probably no longer remember most of what you learned. As effective as such techniques can be for short-term use, they're more than a little cumbersome. And anyway, most information doesn't lend itself to such simple arrangements; mnemonic techniques like those are a hodgepodge, not a formal system with wide applications.

Given the dreariness of rote memorization, and the ultimate ineffectiveness of most mnemonic tricks, I wouldn't be surprised if you've concluded that memorization is something you've given up for good.

But I'm going to try to convince you that memorization itself is not one of those childish ways. In fact, there are methods for memorization — tried and tested for thousands of years — that go far beyond the rote repetition and acronym techniques of our school days, and these techniques can be very valuable for you in your adult life. In the first part of this book, I compare these ancient memory systems to the stone that the builders rejected that later serves as the cornerstone of a great edifice. The edifice we'll build is one of knowledge and memory.

These techniques come down to us primarily from the ancient Greek poet Simonides and the philosopher Aristotle, from Marcus Tullius Cicero (hailed by some as the most profound and influential thinker of all the ancient Romans), and by two of the most sublime Doctors of the Catholic Church: St. Albert the Great (the "Universal Doctor") and St. Thomas Aquinas, the patron saint of scholars. This memory system is not kids' stuff (although children can be taught to use it), and we'll be applying it to the most relevant information imaginable: the facts, doctrines, persons, and principles of Christ's Church.

You hear a lot about the "fullness" of the Catholic Church: two thousand years of history, piety, and doctrine; of works of art, feats of heroism, and acts of charity. But how much of this fullness have you actually drunk in? This book will show how to absorb more of the Church's riches, by tapping into your underutilized powers of thought and memory. These powers were given to you by God to be used for knowing and loving him better, and the techniques in this book will help you develop them to a degree few modern souls have experienced.

The very exercise of memory techniques such as the ones in this book can also be a noble and edifying experience when their subject matter is profound. St. Albert and St. Thomas explicitly recommended the development of memory as an element of a virtuous lifestyle. The intense focus and concentration that mnemonics calls forth can help us shut out the distractions of the world and direct our attention to higher things.

Will this book really help you "memorize the Faith" as the title promises? In a qualified sense, yes. Naturally the full mystery of the Faith cannot be completely grasped and remembered using *any* system. In its fullness, it exceeds our understanding. God has shown us glimpses through revelation, but even the great saints see only through a glass darkly while here on earth. And to live a life of faith surely requires more than memory, or even deep knowledge, of doctrines and facts. It requires prayer and charity and a relationship with God.

But in an important sense, memory and knowledge of the facts of our religion are necessary precursors to living a complete life of faith. We must also *understand* these Christian principles if we are to *apply and live by them*. But it's hard to think about and apply things you can't remember! Be aware that no less than the *Catechism of the Catholic Church (CCC)* itself exhorts us in paragraph 22 of its prologue to *memorize* essential teachings of the Church.

A Vacuum of Religious Knowledge

In a 1996 book, an interviewer commenting on the state of the Church said, "Knowledge about faith is also gone, as if it had all of a sudden been mysteriously vacuumed up by an alien power." The interviewee relied in part, "You are right. There has been a collapse even in simple religious information. This naturally forces us to ask: What is our catechesis doing? What is our school system doing at a time when religious instruction is so widespread? I think it was an error not to pass on more content."

The book is *Salt of the Earth*. The interviewer was Peter Seewald. The then-cardinal he interviewed is now called Pope Benedict XVI.

And so the most ambitious goal of this book is to play some small part in helping to fill in that information vacuum and correct the lack of emphasis on content so sadly prevalent in religious education today. Too often we neglect the hard facts of our faith; in a world hostile to Christianity, we do this at our peril.

So please bear in mind that the value of this book lies both in its *content* and in its *method*. Not only will it show you how to memorize a great deal of important religious information, but it will also assist you in developing a fuller use of your mental faculties for concentration and meditation, to love and serve the Lord. Further, the powerful new systems of memory techniques you'll learn can be applied to *any* subject matter, to *any* area of your life (as will be made apparent, especially in chapter 28).

St. Thomas saw memory systems as essential to full realization of the virtue of prudence; for to achieve virtuous goals in the future, we must act in the present, guided by the memories of what we have learned in the past. Therefore, I argue that it would be quite prudent for an adult of any age to memorize the Faith with the powerful mnemonic system of St. Thomas Aquinas. And remember, it was St. Paul who exhorted us (as one translation has it) to "keep in memory what I preached unto you" (1 Cor. 15:2).

A NOTE TO YOUNGER READERS

Welcome to this book! If you're a young person, I'm glad you're reading this section first. Here's why.

Adults have some advantages over you when it comes to the kinds of mnemonics (memory systems or techniques) used in this book. For one thing, they've been around longer and will be more likely to be familiar with some of the words I'll be using. But there's no need to worry. That's what dictionaries are for!

But you have some advantages over adults. If you're somewhere between junior high school and college age, that brain you're sitting under is probably in very good shape: sleek and muscular, more flexible than adult minds. You'll be able to draw in new information like a powerful electromagnet. But you must use that power carefully: we don't want our magnets pulling in all kinds of junk — only the good stuff. That takes focus, because the world around us is constantly tempting us to let our attention wander away toward things of little value. That's why I'd like to begin by helping you focus your mind, so you can make the most out of this memory book. I'm going to give you a few tips based on the advice that St. Thomas Aquinas gives to us all in chapter 2.

Organization

We think and remember best when we're organized. But don't fear. I'm not saying you'll have to clean your room to make the most of this book. (But it probably wouldn't hurt!)

The dictionary definition of *organize* is to "pull or put together into an orderly, functional, structured whole," or to "arrange or systematize: organize one's thoughts before speaking." Accordingly, the memory methods in this book will put information to be remembered in *order*, literally in numerical order. They'll serve the *function* of helping you remember, and they'll form a *structured whole* (in fact, the structure will be a house). And you'll learn that these memory systems were indeed first invented by public speakers *to organize their thoughts before speaking!*

What's more, the memory techniques in this book will show you not only how to organize information you want to remember, but even how to organize *your own thinking abilities* in a way that you've never imagined. Imagine your various mental abilities — the ability to pay attention, the ability to form mental visual images, the ability to use language — as a team of powerful horses, and imagine yourself as the charioteer. These horses are not going to take you where you want to go if they're pulling in different directions. You've got to train them to work together. So, before you begin, prepare yourself to rein in those mental powers, and get ready to go faster and farther with them than you ever have before.

Imagination

The memory system I'm going to teach you involves imagining things that sound like or remind you of the things you want to remember. Adults have a small advantage here, because they know more words that sound like things they want to remember. If I, for example, being in excess of 40 years of age, wanted to remember that St. Albert the Great (St. Thomas's teacher) is the patron saint of scientists, I could use the word "metaphysics" and imagine St. Albert talking with a physicist (get it? sounds like "met a physicist") to help me remember, but you could not, because you've never even heard of the word *metaphysics*. (If you have, you have my apologies.)

But don't worry. We won't use difficult words to remember simple things. We'll be using *simple* words to remember *difficult* things. Let's say, for example, that *metaphysics* comes up in your eighth-grade vocabulary lesson (or, more likely, in your college Philosophy 101 class). Imagine that you *met a physicist*, like Einstein with all that white hair. Picture this vividly in your mind. And imagine that you're talking with Einstein about *the very first things that go beyond physics, like the reason there even is a universe with physical laws*. This image will remind you both of what *metaphysics* sounds like, "met a physicist," and what it means (the study of first things beyond physics). If you can grasp that example, after rereading it a time or two, you'll have little trouble understanding the mnemonics in this book. In fact, most will be far simpler.

You also have a big advantage when it comes to imagination. You have a very vivid imagination, don't you? Then you'll have no problem picturing in your head some of the bizarre and wacky scenes that appear in this book. And for the great majority of material in this book, you won't even have to make up the images. I'll do that. You'll just have to picture them in your head.

Concentration

We've got to focus our mental powers to make the most of our memory abilities. This involves removing unnecessary distractions (which, again, might or might not involve cleaning your room). Memory techniques are like an "inner speaking" and an "inner writing." It's hard to memorize things when there are competing voices coming from the television or the stereo. I know that from experience. Some of us today are so used to constant noise that it might be hard to concentrate without it. Still, why not give silent study a try and *then* reward yourself with a movie or some tunes when your memory work is finished?

Concentration takes more than just peace and quiet, of course. Too much peace and quiet, and you might do more snoring than studying. To focus your powers on a mental task, you've got to get excited about it. Can you get yourself psyched up to flex your mental muscles and see what you can do? You just might find that it's actually fun to pump up your powers of memory!

Repetition

There's a very old saying that "repetition is the mother of memory." You can't expect to learn everything in this book in one sitting. We learn best when we learn things in small chunks and then return to those chunks and rehearse or repeat them again and again. Feel free to read this book at your own pace, but don't try to remember too much at once. If you can memorize the contents of one room at a time, or one shorter list within a room, that's just fine. This will be especially important to remember when you come to the Rosary and the books of the Bible, where there are so many things to remember. As they say, "Rome wasn't built in a day."

A NOTE TO HOMESCHOOLERS

Perhaps this book will best serve its mission in the hands of *both* young people and adults working together to memorize the Faith, as is epitomized in a homeschool. If you're involved in homeschooling, know that I'm going to keep you in mind in the pages ahead. If you're a parent, you'll find special tips for introducing these techniques to your children in part 5 of this book. Please note too that the techniques we'll use to memorize the Faith can be used to memorize virtually *any academic subject matter*. I'll provide those details later on.

MEMORY MASTER TIPS AND FACTS

Here's an extra feature. At the end of each chapter, you'll find a box with supplementary information to deepen your understanding of the art of memory. You'll see in the chapters ahead that the memory systems are an art (as well as a science). The boxes will supply extra tips and notes designed to help you apply mnemonic techniques and to help you learn more about memory, not only from the classical and medieval memory masters, but also from modern psychological theory and research.

I'll borrow a bit from the style of St. Thomas's *Summa Theologica* (see chapter 2) by using a question-and-answer format. Note that they're *not* review questions to see whether you remember what's in the chapters. They're questions that *I* will answer. Once you've read the book, however, I would advise you to go back from time to time and see if *you* can answer them.

Memorize the Faith!

(and Most Anything Else)

Part 1

The Stone the Builders Rejected

Chapter 1

How to Use This Book

This book is of a very particular sort. The text and illustrations have been structured in such a way that, if you read slowly and carefully, look at the pictures, and follow the instructions, by the time you finish, you'll be able to remember and name the Ten Commandments, the seven capital sins, the seven virtues, the nine Beatitudes, the seven sacraments, the twenty mysteries of the Rosary, and yes, if you are ambitious enough, even the names of the forty-six books of the Old Testament and the twenty-seven books of the New Testament. And all of these in order, both forward and backward!

You will also be shown how to use your new memory skills to recall the four marks of the Church, the four last things, the five precepts of the Catholic Church, St. Thomas Aquinas's five proofs for the existence of God, the six sins against the Holy Spirit, the seven gifts of the Holy Spirit, the seven spiritual works of mercy, the seven corporal works of mercy, the ten holy days of obligation of the Roman Catholic Church, the twelve Apostles, the twelve fruits of the Holy Spirit, twelve sayings of Jesus (chapter and verse), the fourteen Stations of the Cross, twenty-one great figures in Church history, the twenty-five parts of the cardinal virtues, and the forty-four daughters of the capital sins.

Finally, you'll acquire specialized memory skills to retain any biblical passages of your choice (chapter and verse), to learn Greek and Latin religious terminology, to remember prayers and creeds — in fact, to recall virtually any material you desire.

The subject matter of this book is the most important information in the world (and beyond it) — namely, the Faith. Of course, this book cannot cover everything, so it focuses on a selection of some of the most essential doctrines of the Catholic Church that provide practical guidelines for living a Christian life. For how many of them do you *really* know and remember? Do you know the Ten Commandments? In order? How about the nine Beatitudes from the Sermon on the Mount? The four cardinal and three theological virtues? Or the twenty life events of Jesus Christ represented in the mysteries of the Rosary? If not, what are the odds that you can name the forty-six books of the Old Testament and the twenty-seven books of the New Testament?

For those of us with children or grandchildren: even if those children attend Catholic schools or catechism classes, how well do you think *they* would perform on a test of such knowledge of their own faith? If you spend any time quizzing older children and adolescents about their faith, how well do you think your charges would perform?

Sadly enough, before the release of the English edition of the *Catechism of the Catholic Church* in 1994, a study found that only thirty-one percent of American Catholics could name Matthew, Mark, Luke, and John as the authors of the four Gospels of the New Testament; only thirty-eight percent could identify Jesus as the one who delivered the Sermon on the Mount! That's not encouraging. "Blessed are the ignorant of their faith" was *not* a part of that mountain sermon. Other polls found that a significant percentage of Catholics do not believe essential tenets of the Faith, such as the Real Presence of Christ in the Eucharist (thirty percent).

This is all disconcerting to us, but is it surprising that so few believe the doctrines of the Faith when the flame of our knowledge of the light of faith flickers so dimly and stands so obscured? But what can we do to put fuel in our lamps and cast off the wicker baskets hiding their flames?

As I said earlier, part of this book will be about supplying some of that missing content. You can find much of it in any good catechism, of course, but I'm going to give you something more.

Have you ever finished a good book of nonfiction and been asked by a friend to summarize it? In my experience, that's not always easy. It's one thing to be edified while sitting in the recliner, and another thing to retain that enlightenment once the footrest is retracted and we set forth into the world again. So often, the light quickly dims as our memory fades with time. *But this book is purposefully designed so that you'll be able to recall the gist of what you read, and a good measure of the details, by the time we reach the end.*

How is it possible that you'll be able to remember so much so thoroughly? The cornerstone in the construction of this book is a mnemonic (memory aiding) system built into its very foundation, floors, walls, ceilings, and interior decoration. (You'll see in a bit why I use the architectural metaphor.) The inspiration for this special construction derives from one of the greatest minds in the history of Christianity, the "Angelic Doctor" and "Common Doctor" of the Church, the thirteenth-century Dominican friar St. Thomas Aquinas. In his discussion of memory in his monumental work, the *Summa Theologica*, St. Thomas describes and recommends a powerful ancient memory-training system culled from the writings of the classical Greco-Roman world.

For many years prior to my discovery of St. Thomas's writings, I had studied the popular, ancient, and scientific literature on memory strategies and employed them with groups of all ages. In fact, I completed a master's thesis in 1990 on the use of these strategies with adolescents.

During my doctoral internship in psychology at a medical school's memory and aging clinic, I tested adults' memories and taught memory-improvement techniques to some patients. One man in particular stands out in my recollection. This middle-aged professional had undergone surgical removal of brain tissue from his left temporal lobe to control his epilepsy (a condition that causes the body to shake uncontrollably at times during episodes called seizures). Now, for the vast majority of the population, this particular region of the left side of the brain is essential for retaining new information obtained through the use of language. After eight hours of rigorous neuropsychological testing, it was clear that this man had indeed a severely impaired memory for words. Yet his memory for visual materials (such as shapes, colors, and pictures) was entirely normal.

So I trained this man in a technique much like the one described by St. Thomas Aquinas. I taught him to transform words into mental images and to place the images in a series of imagined locations. (I'll provide the details of the technique very soon.) When he used this technique, his recall of a list of words after a thirty-minute delay was improved from zero out of seven words to nine out of eleven, after just one two-hour session. (My internship director, Dr. Ron Zec, presented the results of this intervention at a national conference on rehabilitation from brain damage in Washington, DC, in 1995.)

From 1994 to 2004, I taught about memory and performed mnemonic demonstrations for my college classes, such as memorizing my forty students' names in one session and memorizing (in forward and backward order) random fifty-digit numbers they called out. I also demonstrated to my students how *they* could use these techniques to memorize in a few minutes a twenty-item list of new psychology terms (terms that would appear on the next exam!).

You don't need a doctorate in psychology to use these techniques. Time and again, more than half of my students recalled all twenty items after one demonstration. (In chapter 29, I'll show you how I demonstrated the technique to my students, and I'll supply the actual words they memorized.) So, the odds are very good that you too will be able to profit from these tried-and-true techniques of memory mastery.

The Art of Memory

In her fascinating book on the ancient history of memory techniques, *The Art of Memory*, Frances Yates notes that St. Thomas includes memory techniques in his discussion of the virtue of prudence, but he provides little detail regarding the material to which it might be applied. Still, she writes, "gradually the idea began to dawn that the Middle Ages might think of figures of virtues and vices as memory images, formed according to the classical rules." Yates also mentions St. Augustine's references to the mnemonic arts, and she muses that

> . . . the glimpses into the memory of the most influential of the Latin Fathers of the Church raise speculations as to what a Christianized artificial memory might have been like. Would human images of "things" such as faith, hope, and charity, and of other virtues and vices, or of the liberal arts, have been "placed" in such a memory, and might the places now have been memorized in churches?[1]

This book in fact creates just such a "Christianized artificial memory," and I think St. Thomas would approve (if not of the end product, then at least of the intent). I'll give you more details as we apply it to the subject matter in the chapters ahead. I'll also show you how you can adapt these memory techniques for the retention of all sorts of knowledge. You could apply them to information in

[1] Frances Yates, *The Art of Memory* (Chicago: University of Chicago Press, 1974), 48.

the *Catechism of the Catholic Church* or in the Bible. You could use them to remember important details in your office or classroom. You could even apply these techniques to something as mundane as your grocery list. (My wife is grateful for that one!)

The main memory system built into this book is simple, straightforward, and effective. Oddly enough, in our modern world of nearly universal formal education it is little known, although it has been around in various adaptations for over 2,500 years. When I have demonstrated these memory techniques to college juniors and seniors, many times I have heard, "Why didn't anybody ever teach us this before?"

That's why I call the first part of the book "The Stone the Builders Rejected." You might recall, from Psalm 18:22 and Luke 20:17, that the rejected stone would become the cornerstone. Historically speaking, the primary memory system of this book (and recently, even memorization itself), has been like a stone neglected and rejected, because its value was not realized. Yet today, it will serve as the cornerstone for the mighty house of memory we'll construct within these pages.

For Every Memory, a Place

The main memory system I'm going to teach you is called *the method of loci*. This technique allows you to enhance greatly your ability to remember by employing the powerful faculty of visual imagination and by using what is simple and familiar to recall what is complex and new. In this book I'll help you to create vivid mental images of the information you wish to remember and to place these images in a setting as familiar as your own home. As you walk through the rooms of this house that we'll mentally build, we'll put things like the Commandments, sins, virtues, the Beatitudes, the sacraments, the mysteries of the Rosary, and the books of the Bible in their proper places, so you'll always be able to find them when you need them.

To build any house, we must have tools. The main tools I'll use to help you memorize the essentials of the Faith are provided in St. Thomas Aquinas's master work, the *Summa Theologica (ST)*. Although he presents them there very briefly, in just a few paragraphs, we'll make the most of Thomas's memory tools, and we'll also add some new ones to our tool belts. To introduce you to these memory tools, I'll start with a story that predates even St. Thomas by almost two thousand years.

The ancient Greeks told of a man who once hosted a grand banquet for prominent men of his city, featuring entertainment by the famous poet Simonides. Before his oration, Simonides dedicated the performance to the host and also to the twin gods Castor and Pollux. Upon hearing this dedication, the ungracious host informed Simonides that he would pay him only half his fee, and that he could obtain the other half from Castor and Pollux! Midway through his oration, two young men informed the doorkeeper that Simonides was needed for an emergency. Simonides ran from the building, but could not find the two young men. While Simonides was out, an emergency did indeed arise: the building collapsed, killing the guests as the banquet-hall roof crashed down on top of them. The bodies were so mangled that their own relatives could not identify them. Simonides, however, found that he could. From his perspective as an orator he had seen where each person reclined. By going from couch to couch in his mental image of the audience, he was able to name every man in order.

As the story goes, who were the men who called him away? Yes, Castor and Pollux. And what was Simonides's payment? Yes, his life, but also his discovery of the memory technique that's called today the method of loci. Tradition has retained the Latin word *loci*, from which the English word *location* derives, rather than the Greek word *topoi*, probably because it was the work of later Roman writers (including Cicero), who first made this system known to later European thinkers (including St. Thomas Aquinas).

Simonides discovered that the ability to form visual images is a powerful feature of our natural memory abilities. But more important, he also discovered that we can purposely improve on our *natural* memory abilities by employing a system of *artificial* memory, based on mental visual imagery. In other words, not only do we naturally tend to remember things easily by seeing them in their locations (a feature of natural memory), but we remember things we have seen even better, *including things we have never actually seen*, by simply *imagining* them in particular locations. This is what artificial memory is all about. Let's give it a try right now. Please read this with care and set your imagination on "high."

Welcome to the House of Memory

Imagine that you've just entered someone's house for the first time. (It's a sprawling ranch house in an older neighborhood full of mature maples and oaks.) You ring the bell, the *front door* opens, you're nearly blinded by a powerful light, and you hear a thunderous crash. (Quite an entrance, huh? But we're just getting started.)

You step in, look down at your feet, and you see that the *mat* in front of the door is talking. Not only is it talking; it is cursing very angrily. Next, you notice a *clear glass panel* next to the door and you look outside at the most beautiful, sunny day you've ever seen. Facing back into the house, you're surprised to see an enormous *portrait of your own parents* on the wall on your right. On the adjacent wall, oddly enough, is a *gun rack* secured with a giant padlock. In *the middle of the foyer* you spy an unfamiliar adult, hiding his face with the collar of his shirt. You glance up at the massive *chandelier* over your head, and you notice it's made of solid steel. Turning to your left, you catch your reflection in a *mirror* on the wall, but your image is all distorted, as if you were in a carnival house of mirrors. Below the mirror, on a *small cushioned bench*, you see a familiar face, for there sits the wife of your next-door neighbor. You notice that *drawers in the bench* stand half open, brimming with packages.

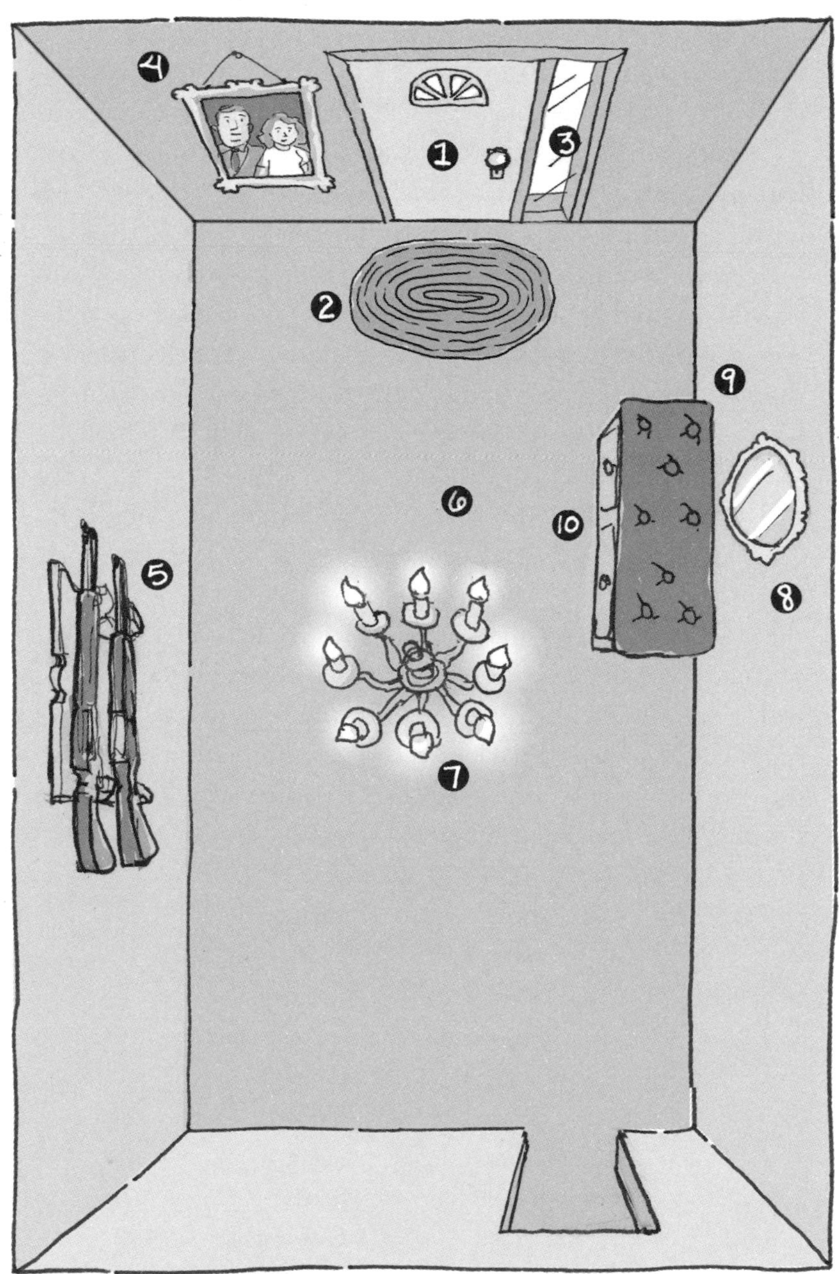

Foyer

Now, when I was young and would say something outlandish, my mother would often say to me, "What's that got to do with the price of beans?" (She came from a family of farmers.) In this case it's a fair-enough question: what did that strange scene in the entranceway have do to with the price of beans, or better yet, with learning anything essential to Christian living?

Let's review this scene again. Can you see this strange scene in your imagination? Here are the locations: 1) the front door, 2) the doormat, 3) the glass panel next to the door, 4) the portrait on the wall, 5) the gun rack, 6) the center of the foyer, 7) the chandelier overhead, 8) the mirror on the opposite wall, 9) the bench under the mirror, and 10) the drawers in the bench.

Next, let's look at the strange visual images associated with those locations. When you open the front door you see *a great light* and hear a great crash. The mat under your feet is *cursing*. Through the glass panel you see the *most glorious day*. The portrait on the wall portrays *your own parents*. Next to that portrait is the gun rack with a huge *padlock*. In the center of the foyer is the secretive *adult*. The chandelier is made of *steel*. The mirror reflects a *false image*. On the bench is your next-door *neighbor's wife*. Finally, the drawers of the bench are full of *packages*. Let's lay this out.

Location	**Image**
1. Front door	*Bright light*
2. Doormat	*Cursing*
3. Glass panel	*Glorious day*
4. Portrait	*Parents*
5. Gun rack	*Padlock*
6. Center of foyer	*Adult*
7. Chandelier	*Steel*
8. Mirror	*False image*
9. Bench	*Neighbor's wife*
10. Drawers	*Packages*

So far, so good? If you now know these ten locations and associated images, that's great! If not, repeat them a few times until you have them, until you can *picture them vividly in your mind's eye*. Got them? Good. If you do, you're very close to knowing and retaining the Ten Commandments, in order. Let's see how close we are.

Do you see what we've done? Each of those strange visual images was used to represent and remind us of one of the Ten Commandments. The light represents God, of course. We even threw in an imagined *sound*: a thunderous crash to represent the destruction of idols to false gods once we've seen the light of the true Lord. The fact that the doormat was cursing reminds us of the second commandment, prohibiting the use of God's name in vain. The glorious day outside is a pretty straightforward reminder of keeping holy the Lord's Day. Also self-explanatory are the portrait of our parents reminding us to honor our parents (fourth commandment) and the *locked* gun rack reminding us of the prohibition of killing (fifth commandment). The secretive *adult* reminds us of adultery (sixth commandment).

The steel chandelier image is a bit different. Here the simple fact that the word *steel* sounds the same as *steal* (and is easier to imagine) allows it to serve as an aid in remembering the seventh commandment prohibiting stealing. The *false* or distorted image in the mirror is a reminder of the eighth commandment against distorting the truth by bearing false witness toward others. The *next-door neighbor's wife* on the bench is again a very literal visual reminder, this time of the ninth commandment against coveting your neighbor's wife. Finally, the *packages* in the drawers, of course, represent for us our neighbor's goods, which we're commanded not to covet.

Placing the visual images in imagined locations is at the core of the *method of loci*. Once you've memorized a set of locations (like our ten locations within the foyer), those same locations can be used again and again for the same or new information. As I said before, you could use them for your grocery list one week, then again next week and every week thereafter with completely different lists, if you like. In this book, we'll employ a total of sixty specific, everyday, easy-to-picture locations to represent hundreds of essential elements of the Faith and guides to Christian living. And as I mentioned before, by the time we've learned them, *we will remember them both forward and backward.*

Speaking of which, if I mention the packages (goods) in the drawers of the couch, can you work your way backward through the neighbor's wife on the bench, the distorted image (false witness) in the mirror, the steel (stealing) chandelier, the secretive adult (adultery) in the center of the foyer, the locked gun rack (killing), the portrait honoring your parents, the glorious day outside (Lord's Day), the cursing doormat, and the incredible light at the front door? If not, rehearse them again, and give it another try. When you can name all ten in order, you'll find that you know the Ten Commandments, literally both forward and backward. The method of loci makes for a very organized memory.

Later, when you master this system, you can create your own locations, as well as any visual images of your choice. But since you're just getting started, I'll supply *all* the images and locations until we've just about come to the end. I'll simply note for now that the mental images you create yourself can be even more powerful, since they're based on associations that pop into *your* own head in the first place. Nonetheless, those provided here should get the job done! I simply ask that you pay attention and persevere. Perseverance, by the way, is one of the parts of the virtue of fortitude, which we'll address in a later chapter. Indeed, you'll see that fortitude itself is located right in the center of the dining-room table (if I recall correctly).

This system might well seem strange to you. But, in fact, the oddness of the images is one thing that makes them so memorable. Hear St. Thomas Aquinas himself on this one: "First, when a man wishes to remember a thing, he should take some suitable yet unwonted illustration of it, since the unwonted strikes us more, and so makes a greater and stronger impression on the mind" (*ST*, II-II, 49, 1). If you're not sure that you want such "unwonted" (strange and unusual) images floating around in your head forever, I assure you that once you've learned tenets of the Faith thoroughly by this system, you'll find that you can recall them *without* the mental locations and *without* the strange visual images. I've employed the first set of locations I ever learned (based on twenty parts of a car) for hundreds, if not thousands of sets of information, and my mental car is *not* brimming over with tens of thousands of images! It's nice and clean every time I go back to it. Further, the important sets of information it helped me retain continue to survive, as long as I bring them to mind again every so often.

In this book we will mentally construct an imaginary house with a foyer, a living room, a dining room, a family room, a study, and a most unusual extra: not cathedral ceilings but a full-blown cathedral! We'll store in this house hundreds of facts and principles essential to our Christian faith. And I almost forgot: we'll employ none other than St. Thomas Aquinas himself, the patron saint of scholars, to guide us on our tour through this holy house.

And please bear in mind that although the images we use might be odd, silly, or fantastic at times, they by no means make light of the sacred ideas they help us remember. Indeed, the use of fantastic images to help us recall profound truths should not be new to Christians. Have you ever tried to form an image of a camel going through the eye of a needle . . . or, better yet, of straining out a gnat and swallowing a camel (Matt. 19:24; 23:24)?!

Memory Overload?

Maybe you're concerned that techniques such as this will overwhelm your memory and send it heading for the hills. After all, remembering the Ten Commandments is work enough, without adding another ten places *and* ten strange images too. But bear a few things in mind. The artificial memory is a *trained* memory, and memory training is not unlike physical training. The individual who takes up weightlifting finds that weights which feel bone-crushing at first soon become child's play. So too with these mnemonics. When you train with them for a while, their burden becomes progressively lighter. And like the lifter who soon goes searching for extra plates to load on the bar, you might soon be seeking out more difficult memory challenges.

More important, after you've made the initial investment to learn the locations, you can use them again and again until kingdom come. They'll become automatic, taking virtually no time or effort to employ. You'll know them inside and out and will have no need to look at a picture.

The creation of vivid mental images will also become easier with practice. You'll have then acquired a nearly automatic system for storing information in your memory and for pulling it back out when you need it. A few weeks of hard work with these techniques could yield a lifetime of greater ease and competence in remembering anything of your choosing.

MEMORY MASTER TIPS AND FACTS

QUESTION 1

What is the great secret of the memory masters?

The memory masters you'll meet in the pages had far more than just clever memory techniques. They also acquired vast knowledge about *how memory works*. Modern psychologists have coined the term *metamemory* to refer to a person's *knowledge about memory* and anything related to storing and recalling information. As you read this book, not only will your memory powers grow, but so will your metamemory. Perhaps you too will become a memory master one day!

Chapter 2

The Memory System of St. Thomas Aquinas

"Grant to me keenness of mind,
capacity to remember,
skill in learning, subtlety to interpret,
and eloquence of speech.
May You guide the beginning of my work,
direct its progress,
and bring it to completion."

From St. Thomas's prayer
Ante Studium ("Before Study")

"Because he had the utmost reverence
for the Doctors of antiquity, he seems to have
inherited in a way the intellect of all."

Leo XIII on St. Thomas Aquinas,
Aeterni Patris, 1879

The Italian poet Dante used his great Roman predecessor Virgil to guide readers through the supernatural realms of his *Divine Comedy*. Now it's time to meet *our* guide, the man who inspired this "Christianized artificial memory" system: St. Thomas Aquinas. As you might have gathered from the quotation from Pope Leo XIII above, St. Thomas comes highly recommended. Many great pontiffs have sung his praises. Allow me to provide just one more example, from Pope John XXII in 1323:

> Accordingly, just as it was said to the Egyptians of old in time of famine, "Go to Joseph," so that they should receive a supply of corn from him to nourish their bodies, so we now say to all such as are desirous of the truth, "Go to Thomas" and ask him to give you from his ample store the food of substantial doctrine wherewith to nourish your souls unto eternal life.

Indeed, let's go to Thomas right now. Thomas Aquinas lived from approximately 1225 to 1274. He was canonized in 1323 and designated a Doctor of the Church in 1567. The privileged seventh child of an Italian lord, and a relative of the imperial family, Thomas nonetheless sought the robe of a poor Dominican friar, to live his life as a preacher and teacher. He bore the gift of a marvelously powerful intellect, exercised it to its fullest, and dedicated and directed it toward the highest possible object: God. Thomas believed fully in the divine revelation that God has given us in the sacred Scriptures. He was also a great champion of human reason (for he reasoned that God endowed us with reason for a reason).

> For when a man's will is ready to believe, he loves the truth he believes, he thinks out and takes to heart whatever reasons he can find in support thereof; and in this way human reason does not exclude the merit of faith but is a sign of greater merit (*ST*, I-II,1,10).

Thomas drew on the vast stores of human knowledge from the ancient Greek and Roman philosophers, as well as Jewish and Muslim philosophers and theologians. Although he borrowed from both natural and supernatural sources, unlike some other theologians of his day St. Thomas maintained there is only *one truth:* that reason cannot lead us to a truth that contradicts the truth provided by revelation. Further, St. Thomas wrote that faith is the ultimate foundation of our life in God here on earth (until it is replaced by direct knowledge of God in heaven).

We are greatly blessed by the fact that St. Thomas wrote prolifically in his less than fifty years on earth. His writings include commentaries on books of the Bible, of Church Fathers, and of philosophers such as Aristotle, as well as three grand summaries or "Summas." St. Thomas's *magnum opus*, his ultimate masterpiece, his monumental summary of theology is the *Summa Theologica*.

The *Summa Theologica* contains thirty-eight treatises, each in itself a full-scale book by modern standards. The three major divisions of the *Summa* are devoted to God, Creation, and Christ, respectively, and they cover an incredibly broad range of topics. The *Summa* is constructed in a very unique and formal way. As noted, there are three major *parts* (and the second part is subdivided into two parts of its own). Each part addresses a series of *questions* (the parts include hundreds of questions), and each question is divided into several more specific *articles*. Each article, in its turn, is started by the presentation of a few objections to St. Thomas's actual stand on each issue. After presenting the objections, including reference to the biblical or other sources from which they derive, Thomas then states, "*On the contrary*," and provides a paragraph or so in which he typically includes a quotation in support of his conclusion. Next, he states, "*I answer that*" and proceeds to give his own reasoned conclusions. Not finished yet, he replies to each one of the objections he presented at the start, typically revealing how the objection presented an incomplete or misconstrued interpretation of the scriptural or philosophical passage it was based on. Talk about thorough!

And so, when I cite a quotation from the *Summa Theologica*, it will look something like this: *ST*, II-II, 49, 1. This would refer to the second part of the second part, the forty-ninth question, first article. In this particular example, the article title is "Whether Memory Is a Part of Prudence."

St. Thomas: Medieval Memory Master

So grand is the *Summa Theologica* in its construction and scope that it has been called a Gothic cathedral of words. There's also reason to believe that *the manner in which it was written* is as incredible as its contents, and this pertains to the powerful trained memory of its author. In *The Book of Memory*, English professor Mary Carruthers focuses on the role of memory in medieval culture, and both St. Thomas and his teacher Albertus Magnus (St. Albert the Great) figure prominently. In a fascinating opening passage, Carruthers compares descriptions of Albert Einstein and St. Thomas Aquinas, written by men who knew them well. Although there are interesting similarities, one relevant difference stands out. While Einstein, in the twentieth century, was praised most highly for the *creativity* that led to his great accomplishments in physics, St. Thomas, in the thirteenth century, was praised most highly for his *memory*. It was said that what he once read and grasped, he never forgot. Carruthers points out that St. Thomas wrote himself notes to aid in dictating his early works to secretaries, but for the *Summa Theologica* such notes have never been found. This leads her to theorize that he simply didn't need them:

> The contemporary sources suggest strongly that the entire *Summa Theologica* was composed mentally and dictated from memory, with the aid at most of a few written notes, and there is no reason to disbelieve them.[2]

Those who are familiar with the *Summa*, or even those who have merely seen it taking up a wide space on a bookshelf, will

[2] Mary Carruthers, *The Book of Memory* (Cambridge: Cambridge University Press, 1990), 5.

appreciate the almost unimaginable powers of memory that would require!

One last note on this issue: It was often reported that St. Thomas spent hours in prayer and meditation before writing on complex themes. His friend Friar Reginald reported that in one instance after doing this, Thomas dictated to him as if he were reading aloud from a book. Considering that trained memory techniques are often referred to as "inner writing," it's quite possible that some of St. Thomas's time in meditation was spent organizing the contents of his prodigious trained memory — "writing" his books in his mind before putting them down on paper.

Aquinas's Work on Memory Forgotten?

Have modern theologians, philosophers, and psychologists overlooked St. Thomas's writings on memory? The most detailed treatments I have seen were written by Mary Carruthers and by a historian named Frances Yates. Apart from those two sources, in reading many insightful modern expositions of St. Thomas's life and writings, I've yet to see his discussion of the art of memory as a part of prudence addressed in any detail. One learned Thomist philosopher even states that the memory of prudence does *not* have anything to do with "mnemo-technical" capacity (that is, with artificial memory techniques). To borrow some terminology from St. Thomas, *on the contrary, I answer that* memory as part of prudence *does* specifically include mnemotechnics — in the explicit words of Thomas himself.

Read the second objection to memory as a part of prudence in the first article of question 49 (II-II): "Further, prudence is acquired and perfected by experience, whereas memory is in us from nature. Therefore memory is not a part of prudence." (Remember, the preceding statement is a *hypothetical objection* that Thomas proceeds to *rebut* — in this case with the lengthiest section of his article on memory.) Citing an ancient Latin text then attributed to Cicero, Thomas replies, "Memory not only arises from nature, but is also aided by art and diligence."

Do you recall from the introduction the distinction between natural and artificial memory? Thomas clearly stands forth as a champion of artificial memory (that which comes from "art and diligence.") Memory has its basis in our human nature, and like the faculties perfected by other virtues, memory too can be perfected by our own habitual actions. But what kind of actions? Thomas proceeds to outline them in four simple steps (let's see if they sound familiar by now):

> There are four things whereby a man perfects his memory.
>
> • First, when a man wishes to remember a thing, he should take *some suitable yet unwonted illustration of it*, since the unwonted strikes us more, and so makes a greater and stronger impression on the mind.
>
> • Secondly, whatever a man wishes to retain in his memory he must carefully consider to *put in order*, so that he may pass easily from one memory to another.
>
> • Thirdly, we must be *anxious and earnest* about the things we wish to remember, because the more a thing is impressed on the mind, the less it is liable to slip out of it.
>
> • Fourthly, we should *often reflect on the things we wish to remember* . . . wherefore when we reflect on a thing frequently, we quickly call it to mind, through passing from one thing to another by a kind of natural order." (II-II,49,1; numerals and emphasis added).

So, in a nutshell (that will soon mature into the full-grown oak of artificial memory), Thomas recommends that we form mental images, place them in a certain order, concentrate on them intently, and rehearse or repeat them often. Seven hundred years and at least as many scientific psychological studies later, any honest modern memory training expert will have to admit that St. Thomas Aquinas got it right!

MEMORY MASTER TIPS AND FACTS

QUESTION 2

What are the parts of metamemory?

The learned men of the Middle Ages were very meticulous in their methods. When they wanted to study something, they would define it and analyze it in detail. The word *analysis*, in fact, derives from Greek words meaning to divide things into parts.

Modern psychologists have analyzed the concept of metamemory and say that it can be divided into three main parts: personal variables, task variables, and strategy variables. *Personal variables* include your knowledge of and awareness of your own memory abilities, of your individual strengths and weaknesses. *Task variables* include your awareness of how the characteristics of different memory tasks contribute to their difficulty. For example, which do you think would be easier to remember: a list of current movie stars or a list of Byzantine emperors? *Strategy variables* include knowledge of techniques or strategies that can be applied to various memory tasks. (If strategy variables sound interesting to you, then you're reading the right book!) Stay tuned for more metamemory in the chapters ahead.

Part 2

As for Me and My House

Chapter 3

The Ten Commandments

"Since they express man's fundamental duties towards God and towards his neighbor, the Ten Commandments reveal, in their primordial content, grave obligations. They are fundamentally immutable, and they oblige always and everywhere. No one can dispense with them. The Ten Commandments are engraved by God in the human heart."

Catechism of the Catholic Church, 2072

We used the Ten Commandments in "How to Use This Book" to illustrate the method of loci, so I won't be presenting the mnemonic tour here. You'll find the Ten Commandments in Exodus 20:2-17 and Deuteronomy 5:6-21. They're covered in great depth in the *Catechism* (over 120 pages' worth) and in various sections throughout the *Summa Theologica.*

Do you know them now, forward and backward? If not, it's time for a little more repetition. Please look at the chart on the following page, and take a moment to review the Commandments, along with the ten locations in the foyer. Here's a last exhortation to remember them:

Write them on the tablet of your heart (Prov. 3:3).

THE TEN COMMANDMENTS

Location	Image	Commandment
1. Front door	*Bright light*	1st: I am the Lord your God; you shall not have false gods before me.
2. Doormat	*Cursing*	2nd: You shall not take the name of the Lord your God in vain.
3. Glass panel	*Glorious day*	3rd: Remember to keep holy the Lord's Day.
4. Portrait	*Parents*	4th: Honor your father and your mother.
5. Gun rack	*Padlock*	5th: You shall not kill.
6. Center of foyer	*Adult*	6th: You shall not commit adultery.
7. Chandelier	*Steel*	7th: You shall not steal.
8. Mirror	*False image*	8th: You shall not bear false witness against your neighbor.
9. Bench	*Neighbor's wife*	9th: You shall not covet your neighbor's wife.
10. Drawers	*Packages*	10th: You shall not covet your neighbor's goods.

MEMORY MASTER TIPS AND FACTS

QUESTION 3

Have there been "Mozarts" of memory mastery?

There have not been child prodigies of memory, as far as I know. There have been rare children with unusually powerful mental abilities, of course — some, for example, who have gone on to college before they reach their teens. It is said that Mozart himself could memorize complex musical pieces after hearing them but once. But memory mastery is about more than intellectual gifts or raw ability. It requires metamemory, a kind of a practical wisdom of memory. And that comes only with time and experience.

Metamemory changes through a predictable course as we develop. For example, five-year-olds have been found to grossly overestimate the number of objects they can recall, and they tend to attribute performance on memory tasks more to their mental abilities than to characteristics of the tasks. Older children with a few years of schooling under their belts have more realistic concepts of their mnemonic abilities. Their predicted recall matches more closely their actual recall. Perhaps this is because in school they repeatedly see their memories put to the test.

Chapter 4

The Seven Capital Sins

"They are called 'capital' because they engender other sins, other vices. They are pride, avarice, envy, wrath, lust, gluttony, and sloth or acedia."

Catechism of the Catholic Church, 1866

Does the idea of "capital sins" seem painfully old-fashioned to you? It does to some people. Well, thinking and talking about capital sins might have gone out of style, but committing them sure hasn't! In our world, where you just have to turn on daytime television to see each of them in action, it's more important than ever to know and understand these sins — so as to avoid them.

Why are these seven sins called "capital"? St. Thomas points out that the word *capital* comes from the Latin word *caput*, meaning "head." When we speak of capital sins, we are using *head* in a metaphorical sense. Who is the "head" of a company or a state or a household? The person in charge, who directs other people; the person who forms the goals, issues the commands, and gets the ball rolling. Thomas notes that St. Gregory compared the capital sins to leaders of an army. In this case, the soldiers are a multitudinous variety of sins and misdeeds, and the capital sins are the officers who set them to their nefarious tasks.

Living Room

The capital sins are discussed in great detail, both as a class and as individual sins, in several places in the *Summa Theologica.* St. Thomas addresses them in his treatise on habits and again in his treatise on virtue when he shows which virtues they oppose. Question 84 of the first part of the second part is entitled "Of the Cause of Sin, in Respect of One Sin Being the Cause of Another." One fascinating aspect of St. Thomas's treatment of these sins is his analysis of the offspring, or "daughters," that are likely to arise from the capital sins. Here's just one example, from his treatment of envy.

Thomas approves of St. Gregory's list of "hatred, tale-bearing, detraction, joy at our neighbor's misfortunes, and grief for his prosperity" as the daughters of envy. He elaborates by noting that envy arouses a struggle within us that unfolds in a sequence. The envious man might begin by trying to harm another's reputation, either secretly through *tale-bearing*, or openly through *detraction.* Later, if his acts of defamation are successful, the envious man will have *joy at another's misfortune*, and if they fail, he will *grieve at another's prosperity*. The end toward which envy drives is *hatred* for our neighbor; for envy is contrary to love.

The Living Room of Deadly Sins

Let's forge ahead now and learn all seven of these "capital" and "deadly" sins. It's time to move out from the foyer and continue to tour the rooms of our mnemonic house.

Imagine that when you look out from the foyer and into the living room, you gaze upon some very unusual sights. Shaken by their unseemliness, you consider heading back through the front door. You're really ready to bolt when you see a large figure heading your way down the hallway, but his serene countenance tells you in an instant that he means no harm. The huge frame, the distinctive friar's robe and haircut, and the massive book in his hands tell you this is none other than St. Thomas Aquinas himself. He informs you that he has learned a great deal from the early Church fathers about the contents of this next room and he will be there to guide you through it. So in you go.

The first location in the living room is the eleventh in our mnemonic house (after the ten hosting the Commandments). It is the *center of that room*, and in the center is a *large statue of you*, surrounded by a *pride of lions*. As you look out the *picture window* (location 12), you see huge *trees growing dollar bills* instead of leaves. Turning toward the *large sofa* (13), you spy one of your neighbors, and his face is a rich shade of *green* that would rival the Incredible Hulk. On the *coffee table* (14) in front of him, you notice a *large damaged Christmas wreath*. Gazing across the room at a *giant television screen* (15), you note that the channel changes every second, and every image features *bikini-clad women*. You turn to the *fireplace* (16) and notice an *entire boar*, complete with an apple in its mouth, roasting on a spit. Finally, Thomas begins to lead you out into the dining room, when you notice your path has been blocked at the *doorway* (17) by a *giant sloth*. When the sloth sees St. Thomas, he rouses himself and lumbers out of the way.

Let's Look at That Again

Perhaps you think I'm moving too fast at this point? That last little paragraph contained the entire mnemonic system for this chapter, and you're new to this technique. Let me point out that as we go through the locations of our house of memory, we'll be forming a mental image at every numbered location. Take your time with these, and allow me to guide you through the first image of this chapter in some detail.

Let's go back to location 11. This is the center of the living room. Once you've learned this system well, whenever you picture that location, you'll know it is the eleventh item on your list, whether the sin of pride, or a book of the Old or New Testament we'll place there later on. For now, just know that we're creating a mental reminder of the sin of pride. We've used a statue of you. Doesn't that suggest a bit of pride? It should help you remember this sin. But note that the images do not have to convey the *meaning* of the word they represent. In fact, many in this book will not. The images simply have to remind us of the word we want to remember. Many are like the second suggestion that I provided — namely, the use of the pride of lions. This works simply because that word is the same as pride, the sin, and because lions are very easy to picture.

Actually, either one of those images alone would work, but since we're just getting started, I supplied both. And of course, many other images would also work. Sometimes people you know or famous figures make very memorable images. For example, I could have placed the singer Charlie Pride in the center of the living room to remind us of pride. When you've mastered this system, you'll be able to apply it to new materials using whatever associations pop into *your* head.

Your most important task is to form a vivid mental picture of these images. This comes more easily to some people than to others, but with practice, it becomes easier for everyone. Vividly picture both the locations and the images. Can you imagine what your statue would look like — your pose, the material, and so forth? Can you imagine the lions, both males and females? Give them as much detail as you need to make them memorable. When you become adept at these techniques through practice, forming these images won't take long. For now, take your time and get used to using your imagination to the max. It will yield memorable rewards later on!

Next, let's review the whole room a second time.

As a glance at the accompanying picture and table will show, the statue of you represents *pride*, and the pride of lions helps us lock in that association. The trees seen out of the window are growing money, and this, of course, reminds us of *avarice* (or greed).

THE SEVEN CAPITAL SINS		
Location	**Image**	**Sin**
11. Center of living room	*Statue of self/pride of lions*	Pride
12. Picture window	*Trees growing money*	Avarice
13. Sofa	*Green man*	Envy
14. Coffee table	*Damaged wreath*	Wrath
15. Big-screen TV	*Bikini-clad women*	Lust
16. Fireplace	*Boar on spit*	Gluttony
17. Living-room doorway	*Giant sloth*	Sloth

The neighbor on the sofa is green with *envy*. *Wreath* sounds like *wrath*, and the fact that it is damaged depicts the kind of destruction that wrath can bring with it. The image of the TV screen flashing bikini-clad women every second (which does not sound at all far-fetched these days) represents *lust*. The boar roasting in the fireplace is our image for *gluttony*, and the slow-moving, furry sloth, of course, is a completely straightforward image for *sloth*.

Please review the picture and the table. Do you know the living room and the seven capital sins now? Can you name them in backward order? If so, let's put those seven capital sins in their place by moving on to a much more virtuous topic: the seven virtues.

MEMORY MASTER TIPS AND FACTS

QUESTION 4

How does IQ differ from metamemory?

For years I've been involved in Mensa, the "high IQ society," because I think human intelligence is very important as a subject of study and as a gift to be employed to the fullest. But believe me, true intelligence is more than just an IQ score. Intelligence is not something you simply *have*; it is also something you *do*, something you can improve and enhance with effort and practice. This includes developing metamemory and intellectual self-discipline. Your mind might be a powerful turbo-charged engine, but if you're just idling, even a bicycle will pass you.

Chapter 5

The Seven Virtues

"And if anyone loves righteousness, her labors are virtues:
for she teaches self-control and prudence, justice and courage;
nothing in life is more profitable for men than these."

Wisdom 8:7

"The object of our inquiry is not to know
what virtue is but how to become good."

Aristotle, *Nichomachean Ethics*, Book II

The seven virtues are divided into two groups: four "cardinal" virtues and three "theological" virtues. The latter — faith, hope, and charity — derive from 1 Corinthians 13:13 and are called "theological" because they have God as both their source and end. The cardinal virtues (from the Latin *cardo*, "hinge") are so called because they're the ones on which all other natural virtues depend.

Our culture desperately needs a resurgence of the cardinal virtues: prudence, justice, fortitude, and temperance. We need people with the *prudence* to guide their lives based on principles and to realize that good ends can never justify evil means. We need people who will give fair due to all, regardless of the high or low status of those who appeal to their *justice*. We need people with the *fortitude* to stand up for their beliefs, regardless of how unpopular they might seem. And we direly need *temperate* parents today, those who can elevate the responsibilities and welfare of their families over the gratifications of their own material desires.

Why are these four called "cardinal" virtues? The word derives from the Latin *cardo*, meaning "hinge." Other virtues depend on them — hang from and swing on them. They were known to the writers of the Old Testament (see the passage from Wisdom at the beginning of this chapter), and the greatest pagan philosophers knew them well and loved them. Their most thorough classical exposition in my opinion is in Aristotle's *Nichomachean Ethics*. St. Thomas thought highly of this book too, having written a commentary on its every line. Cicero's *On Duties* is also a masterful exposition of the cardinal virtues.

Moving from pagan to Christian sources, we find the cardinal virtues briefly addressed in paragraphs 1805 through 1809 of the *Catechism of the Catholic Church*. But the greatest Christian source, to my knowledge, is again the *Summa Theologica*. St. Thomas's deep, extensive treatment of these virtues is peerless. He devotes five hundred pages to them in the second part of the *Summa*!

But the cardinal virtues are by no means the be-all and end-all of virtue. The cardinal virtues are natural virtues, known to man by his own reason. In the Bible we learn of higher, supernatural virtues, the theological virtues infused in us by God. These are faith, hope, and love (charity), and we know from St. Paul which is the greatest. These are the hallmark virtues of Christianity. To study them in the greatest depth, I refer you yet again to the *Summa*. For now, let's tour the dining room to lock all these virtues into place.

Dining with the Virtues

St. Thomas has led you from the living room of the capital sins into the dining room, and as you cross the threshold (location 18) he introduces you to a friend by the nickname of "Prude." You're

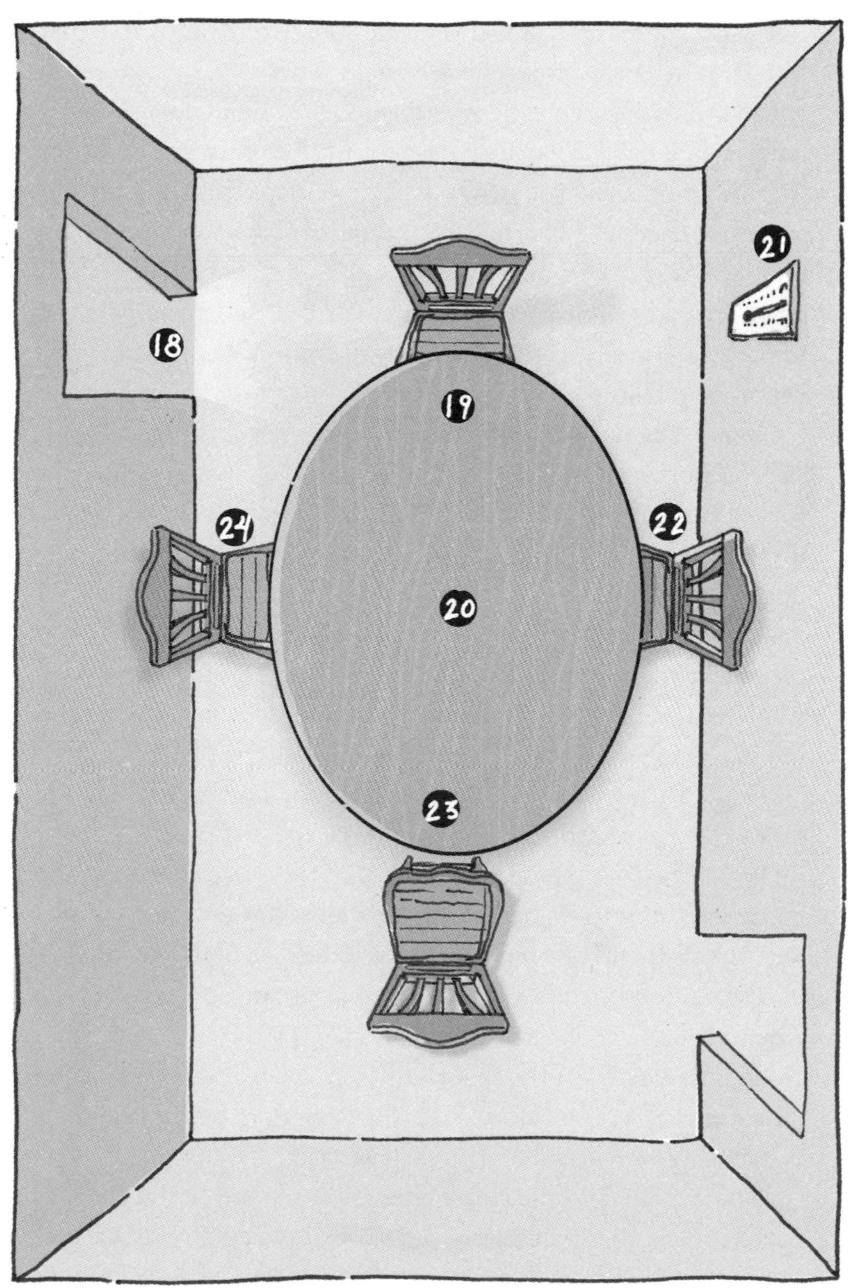

Dining Room

not sure what to think at first. The dictionary, after all, tell us that a prude is "a person, especially a woman, who is overly concerned with being or seeming to be modest, proper, or righteous." Thomas tells you that her real name is *Prudence*. You haven't met a Prudence in quite a while, and you're surprised to see not a stern matron, but a vibrant, cheerful, beautiful young woman. You're surprised even more when you look more closely and notice that Prudence has *three faces*, since she must remember the past and anticipate the future to act wisely in the present. (All three of her mouths happen to be nibbling *prunes*, by the way, just to help you remember the sound of her name, and to remember her virtue of *prudence*.)

The woman welcomes you to the dining room and points out some distinguished guests. At the head of the table (19) sits a *judge* in black robes. He's there to administer justice, since after prudence comes the virtue of *justice*. In the center of the table (20) you notice a massive child's *fort*, conveniently located to help you remember the virtue of *fortitude*. Over on the wall you notice a wall thermometer (21), undoubtedly to record the *temperature* and remind you of the virtue of *temperance*.

Going back to the table you see there are three chairs left, one for each remaining virtue. With all due respect to Prudence's natural beauty, you can't help but notice that the three women in the chairs have a strange glowing beauty that seems to transcend this world altogether. Their names, of course, are *Faith*, *Hope*, and *Charity*, the same as the virtues they represent. Is any other mnemonic needed here? I doubt it. But just in case, picture a glowing *face* (sounds like faith) in the first chair (22), a large *hope chest* at the foot of the table, at location 23, and a *chair with* a cup of *tea* (charity) in the seat on the left, the 24th location.

Now let's review (and please refer to the picture on the previous page). In the doorway, three-faced *Prudence* nibbling *prunes* reminds us of prudence, the *judge* at the head of the table reminds us of *justice*, the *fort* as the centerpiece reminds us of *fortitude*, the

THE SEVEN VIRTUES

Location	Image	Virtue
18. Dining-room doorway	*Prune*	Prudence
19. Head of table	*Judge*	Justice
20. Center of table	*Fort*	Fortitude
21. Thermometer	*Temperature*	Temperance
22. Seat on right	*Face*	Faith
23. Foot of table	*Hope chest*	Hope
24. Seat on left	*Chair with tea*	Charity

temperature of the wall thermometer represents *temperance*, and the *three beautiful sisters* in the chairs (or the *face*, *hope chest*, and *chair with tea*) remind us of *faith*, *hope*, and *charity*. Do we have the four cardinal and three theological virtues down now? Good, be sure to practice them today.

MEMORY MASTER TIPS AND FACTS

Question 5

Isn't repeated exposure sufficient for learning?

You'll find the saying that "repetition is the mother of memory" repeated a few times in these pages, but as St. Thomas has made clear, repetition is only one of four key elements required to perfect artificial memory. Consider how well you remember the details of some things you've seen countless times. Try, for example, to draw the front and back of a penny. How many of the details are in their proper places? Or better yet, without looking, can you draw the lines of your own palms? Plain old repetition is just not enough on its own. We must also pay attention, and to remember difficult things, let's not forget to employ organization and imagination too!

Chapter 6

The Nine Beatitudes

"The Beatitudes are at the heart of Jesus' preaching. They take up the promises made to the chosen people since Abraham. The Beatitudes fulfill the promises by ordering them no longer merely to the possession of a territory, but to the Kingdom of heaven."

Catechism of the Catholic Church, 1716

It is with some reluctance that we prepare to enter the family room, taking our leave of those three graceful sisters of Faith, Hope, and Charity, but St. Thomas assures us that they'll be present in spirit in the rest of the rooms of this house. We have nine stops in the family room. The 25th through 33rd locations in our house will take in those nine keys to blessedness that Jesus gave us in the greatest of sermons. We'll remember key words to remind us of all nine keys to his kingdom.

To meditate on the Beatitudes in Jesus' own words, see the fifth chapter of Matthew. See also the *Catechism* (1716-1729). For St. Thomas's interpretation, the *Summa Theologica* (I-II, 69) is the place to go.

Now please prepare to rev up your imagination. I encourage you to take a good look at the family room's blueprint before we get started, just to make yourself "at home."

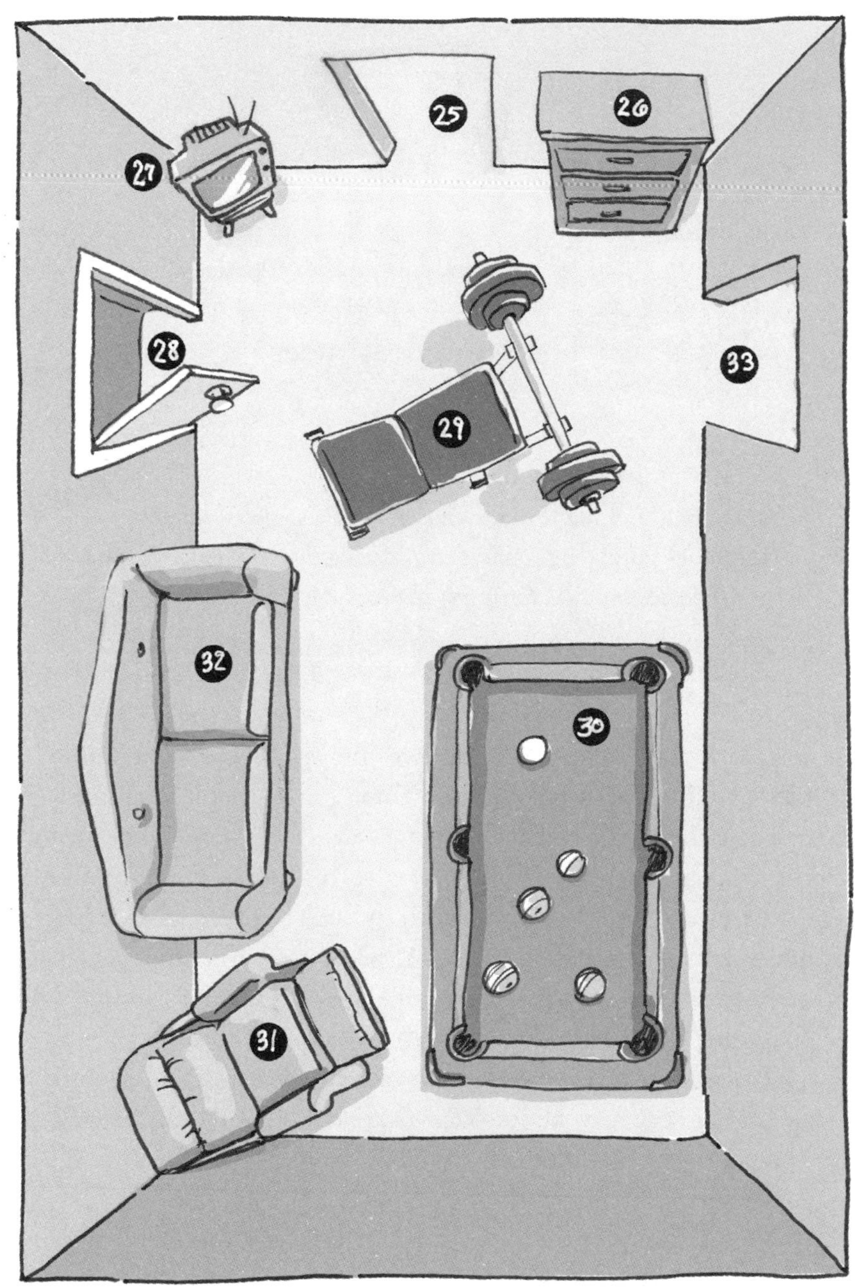

Family Room

Blessed Is This Family Room

When you open the door into the family room, the 25th location, you're met by the outstretched hand of the *ghost of a beggar* in rags. But he isn't sad; nor is asking for alms at the moment. He's excited for the opportunity to show you what lies ahead in this room. The spectral beggar, by the way, represents the first of the nine Beatitudes, *poverty of spirit.* As you enter the family room, you notice a tall dresser (location 26) in the corner right next to the door. There's another person sitting on top of it, and this person *is* sad: all dressed in black is a woman in *mourning*, for the second beatitude speaks of mourning. On the other side of the door, in our 27th location, is a small television, and sitting on top is a small animal with incredibly shiny and beautiful fur. This is a *mink*, and the mink's job is to remind us of *meekness*.

Next, you hear a moaning noise from a large closet next to the television (location 28). You open the door and are astonished to see the skeletal frame of a *starving person* on the *right*. This is just an image, of course, to remind us of *hunger for righteousness*, the fourth of the Beatitudes. There's another alarming scene at location 29. Here is a weight-lifting bench, and a man is trapped under a loaded barbell. You hurry over to help pull the bar off his chest.

You notice that this heavily muscled man is wearing a French beret, and when you help him, he booms out, "*Merci!*" This French word of thanks will help us recall the beatitude of *mercy*.

Location 30 is an eight-foot pool table, and oddly, instead of a wooden triangle containing the rack of billiard balls, there's a large wooden *heart*, for the sixth beatitude concerns *purity of heart*.

The next site (31) is a cozy, comfortable *recliner*, and it makes you think peaceful, relaxing thoughts, not just because it's a recliner, but also because there is a huge *peace-sign design* on the back of the chair: the seventh beatitude regards *peacemaking*.

Next to the recliner is a couch (32), and on it sits a great *grizzly bear* holding quite primly a woman's stylish *purse*. This might seem odd, but it's ever so logical, since the eighth beatitude entails *bearing persecution*.

Finally you arrive at the door, location 33. You find that the door is stuck shut. The bear gets off the couch to open it for you. When her great paws send the door flying open, you hear a great crash and see a large puddle on the ground, because the door had been blocked with a huge vial of liquid. The *bear* and the *vial*, you see, will help us recall the ninth beatitude, that of *bearing reviling*.

THE NINE BEATITUDES

Location	Image	Beatitude
25. Doorway to family room	*Ghost of beggar*	Poverty of spirit
26. Dresser	*Mourner*	Mourning
27. Television	*Mink*	Meekness
28. Closet	*Starving person*	Hunger for righteousness
29. Weight bench	*Struggling lifter: "Merci!"*	Mercy
30. Pool table	*Heart-shaped ball rack*	Purity of heart
31. Recliner	*Peace sign*	Peacemaking
32. Couch	*Bear with purse*	Bearing persecution
33. Doorway out	*Bear and vial of liquid*	Bearing reviling

Do you have them down, every last blessed one? If not, rehearse them a few times, for even with a mnemonic system, *repetition is the mother of memory*. And be sure to turn to Matthew 5 to enjoy in full his rendering of the Beatitudes. Then, when you're ready to move on, I invite you to inspect the most extraordinary room of our mnemonic house.

MEMORY MASTER TIPS AND FACTS

QUESTION 6

Which is better, distributed or undistributed learning?

Distributed learning refers to learning that's stretched out and repeated over time. Undistributed learning is that furious frenzy of panicked, last-minute learning that we call "cramming." Well, distributed learning wins. Repetition or rehearsal works best when it is stretched out over time. Formal research studies have shown this, but most of us probably also realize this from experience. (Actually, when faced with a tough examination, I use both!)

Chapter 7

The Seven Sacraments

"The whole liturgical life of the Church revolves around the Eucharistic sacrifice and the sacraments. There are seven sacraments in the Church: Baptism, Confirmation or Chrismation, Eucharist, Penance, Anointing of the Sick, Holy Orders, and Matrimony."

Catechism of the Catholic Church, 1113

We've left the family room of our mnemonic house and come upon an amazing architectural wonder. This next room is not merely a room, but a complete cathedral, a house of God. This is all and well, considering its unique contents. The other subjects of this book can be studied on your own and practiced in the course of your daily life. But the subject of *this* chapter requires a Church — yes, the church building, but more important, the Church as the body of Christians, the followers of Christ. Our subject is the sacraments.

Our understanding of the sacraments is based on a wealth of biblical texts and a long and rich tradition within the Church. They are masterfully explained in the *Catechism of the Catholic Church* and unpacked in the third part of St. Thomas's *Summa Theologica*. Let's see what's in our mnemonic cathedral.

Imagine that as the door to the cathedral opens, you're awed by the beauty and sanctity of what lies within. Make it as large and as

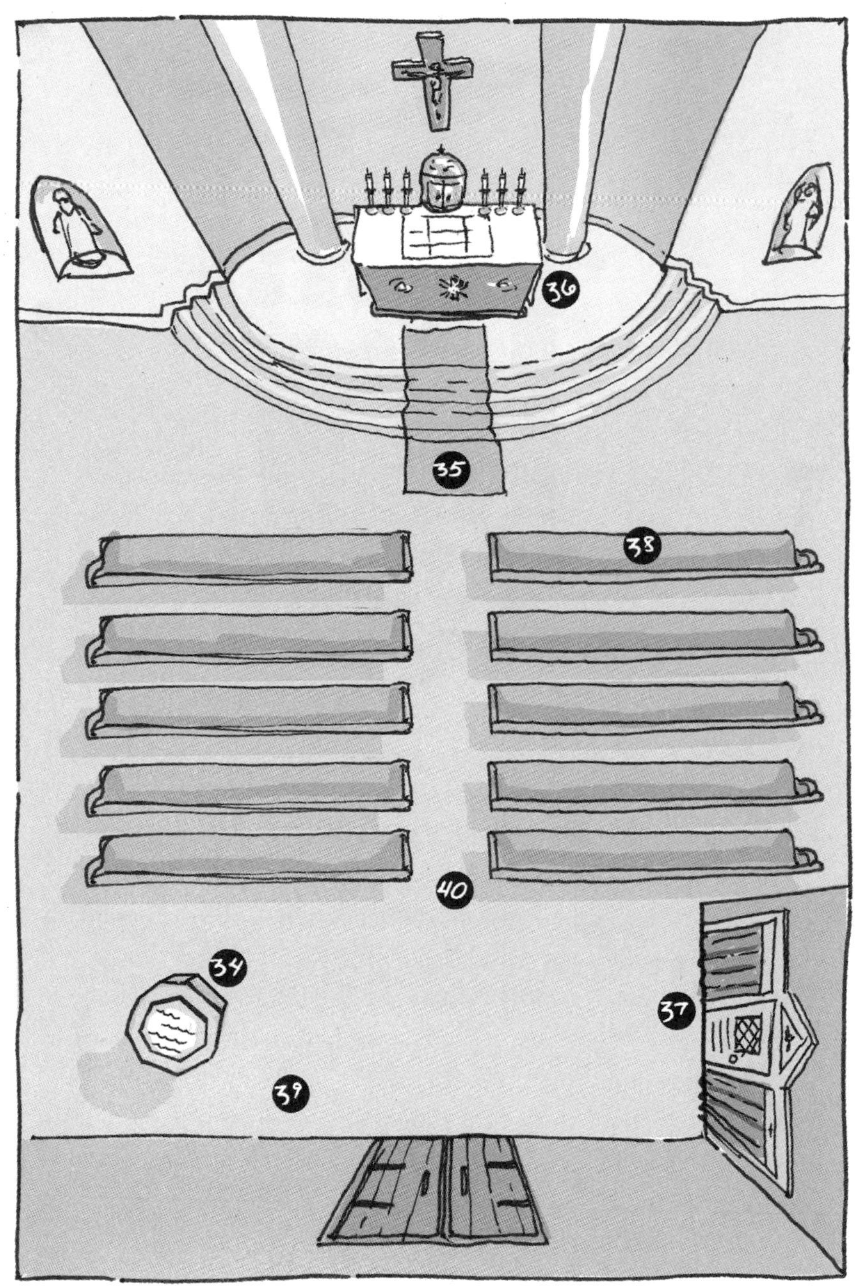

Cathedral

beautiful as possible; it's the "House of God" as tended to by the Church, the "Bride of Christ." As you open the door to our mnemonic cathedral, your attention is first drawn to the baptismal font at location 34. And who should be splashing about there but *John the Baptist* himself. He's certainly not just splashing, though; he's performing what he's best known for, a *baptism*. Can you picture the eyes of a newborn staring in wonder at this great saint?

Next, center front (location 35), is *your bishop*. He's exhibiting great *concentration*, for he's there for a solemn occasion, the sacrament of *Confirmation*. Picture the pews full of eighth-graders waiting to receive this sacrament. At location 36, the altar, is a priest, St. Thomas Aquinas himself, saying, "*You Christ*" as he holds aloft the *Eucharist*, under the appearance of a wafer of bread.

Along the wall you spy a confessional box (location 37), and you notice that it's decorated with baseball-team *pennants*, for the confessional with pennants represents the sacrament of *Penance*. At the front of the right row of pews (location 38) is an enormous amphora of oil, for the fifth sacrament is the *Anointing of the Sick* (formerly called Extreme Unction). Next (location 39), at the back of the church, under a massive mosaic of the risen Christ, sits *your bishop again*, and he seems to be *giving out orders*. In fact, that's exactly what he's doing, for the sixth sacrament is *Holy Orders*.

Finally, you hear an unmistakable tune, "*Here Comes the Bride*," and here (location 40) comes the most *beautiful bride* you've ever seen, clad in a white gown, preparing to ascend the aisle, with her father at her side. The last sacrament, then, is *Matrimony*.

St. Thomas tells us that earlier theologians had related each of the seven sacraments to one of the seven virtues. These relations could provide a starting point for meditations on both sets of seven for those who have committed both sevens to memory:

> They say that Baptism corresponds to Faith, and is ordained as a remedy against Original Sin; Extreme Unction, to

THE SEVEN SACRAMENTS

Location	Image	Sacrament
34. Baptismal font	*John the Baptist*	Baptism
35. Center front	*Your bishop*	Confirmation
36. Altar	*"You Christ"*	Eucharist
37. Confessional	*Pennants*	Penance (Reconciliation)
38. Front pew right	*Amphora of oil*	Anointing of Sick
39. Back of church	*Your bishop*	Holy Orders
40. Start of the center aisle	*Beautiful bride*	Matrimony

Hope, being ordained against venial sin; the Eucharist, to Charity, being ordained against the penal effect which is malice; Order, to Prudence, being ordained against ignorance; Penance to Justice, being ordained against mortal sin; Matrimony to Temperance, being ordained against concupiscence (*ST*, III, 65, 1).

I've culled out the sacrament/virtue parallels for you:

The Seven Sacraments	**The Seven Virtues**
Baptism	Faith
Anointing of the Sick	Hope
Eucharist	Charity
Holy Orders	Prudence
Penance	Justice
Confirmation	Fortitude
Matrimony	Temperance

MEMORY MASTER TIPS AND FACTS

Question 7

What are "flashbulb memories"?

Some memories are so striking to us that they're seemingly stored forever as if photographed, bypassing the normal steps of processing information. Researchers have studied people's memories like this by asking them if they can remember things such as where they were when President Kennedy was shot, when the space shuttle Challenger exploded, or on the morning of 9/11. Surely you have events in your personal life, both bad and good, that you know you'll never forget. Here's what Aristotle said about "flashbulb" memories (over two thousand years before cameras):

> There are some movements by a single experience of which persons take the impression of custom more deeply than they do by experiencing others many times; hence, upon seeing some things but once, we remember them better than others which we may have seen frequently (*On Memory*, ch. 2).

Chapter 8

The Twenty Mysteries of the Rosary

"The Church's devotion to the Blessed Virgin is intrinsic to Christian worship. . . . The liturgical feast dedicated to the Mother of God and Marian prayer, such as the Rosary, an 'epitome of the whole Gospel,' express this devotion to the Virgin Mary."

Catechism of the Catholic Church, 971

The format for this chapter will be a little different from the others so far. The images we use here are very special ones. As much as possible, we will create mental images that reflect the actual scenes of Christ's life commemorated in the mysteries of the Rosary. The Rosary is already an image-based mnemonic device of sorts, so what better images than the real ones? Hence, I'll provide just a little of the commentary up front, and let the mnemonic images speak for themselves a page or two down the road.

My earliest memories of the Rosary take me back to the beloved Dominican sisters who taught me in grade school. The Rosary attached to the belts of their classic black-and-white habit was far more than a fashion accessory. It boldly attested to their devotion to Christ and his Mother.

Recitation of the Rosary is a powerful devotional and meditational tool. It helps us withdraw from the distractions of the world to focus on far higher things. It shows respect to the Mother of God, echoing the words of the angel Gabriel and of St. Elizabeth in the Gospel of Luke. It asks for Mary's help, as the model of perfect prayer (CCC, 2679), and it draws our minds to the loving deeds of Christ on earth.

If recited regularly, the Rosary also builds our capacities for imagination and concentration. Repetition and organization are key components in its very construction. The creation of the Rosary is yet another reason we stand in debt to those devout medieval masters of memory (and of course, to the Virgin Mary!).

Repetition of the prayer we call the Hail Mary forms the spoken background, like a chant, of meditations on events in the life of Jesus. The ultimate focus of the Rosary, then, is on Jesus Christ. In fact, the *Catechism* calls the Rosary an "epitome of the whole Gospel." An epitome is an especially representative summary. The Rosary itself, then, has actually functioned as a powerful mnemonic for the key events of the Gospel since the time of St. Dominic, in the Middle Ages. (St. Thomas, by the way, addresses the medieval form of the Hail Mary in *The Aquinas Catechism*.)

The Rosary has traditionally consisted of three groups of "mysteries": the Joyful Mysteries of Christ's early life, the Sorrowful Mysteries of his Passion, and the Glorious Mysteries of life after his resurrection. In our time, Pope John Paul II proclaimed a group of Luminous Mysteries — mysteries of light. These focus on Jesus as light to the world in the events of his social ministry.

So, without further ado, let's move into the study as we learn the twenty greatest mystery stories ever revealed to man.

THE FIVE JOYFUL MYSTERIES (41-45)

Imagine at location 41, as you open the door to the study, you're met by an ecstatic Dominican *nun!* She's of the same religious order as St. Thomas Aquinas, so picture her wearing the familiar black and white habit. She looks as if she has seen an angel,

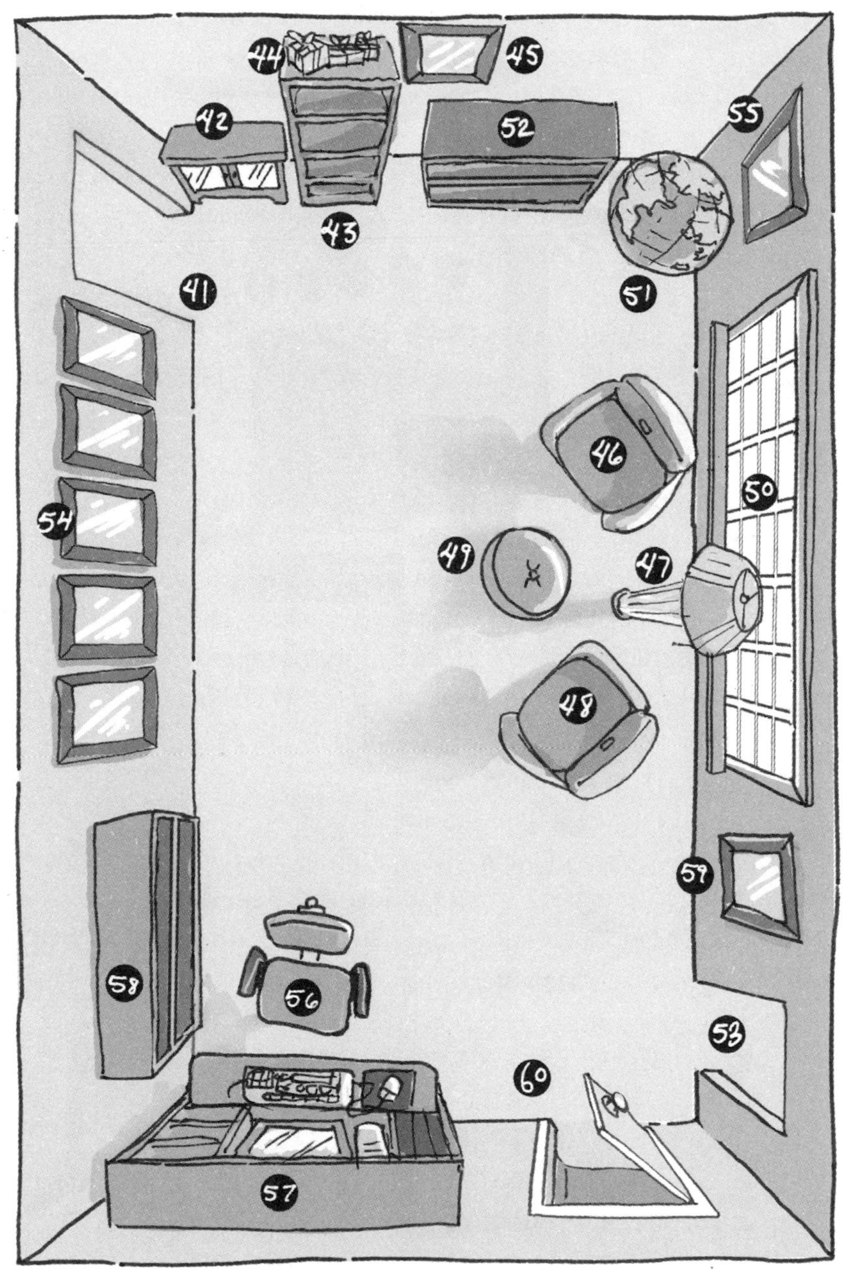

Study

and she has, because the first joyful mystery is the *Annunciation*. Do you recall the scene with the angel Gabriel and the Virgin Mary? This is it: the Annunciation, the announcement that she is to bear the Savior.

As you enter the room, you notice a small glassed-in bookcase (location 42). Inside it you see a "*Visitor's Information*" sign, and you realize that you're witnessing a very special scene. Mary is visiting her cousin Elizabeth, as also related by St. Luke. Do you recall that Elizabeth's baby (St. John the Baptist) jumped in her womb in the presence of the pregnant Mary? This is the joyful mystery of the *Visitation*.

Next to the small bookshelf, in the 43rd location, is a very tall bookcase, and it makes you think of Christmas. Why? Because its top shelf contains the most beautiful *Nativity scene* you ever saw. Why? Because the third joyful mystery is the birth of Christ, the *Nativity*. On top of that tall bookcase is a statue, our 44th location. Perhaps it strikes you as a little odd to see a bronze statue of *a gift-wrapped present*, but it represents the most special of presents, the scene where Mary and Joseph present the baby Jesus in the Temple. The mystery is the *Presentation*.

Please keep the Temple in mind, because above and to the right of the statue, in our 45th location, is another portrait, this one of Jesus himself, as a child, inside that Temple. Imagine Joseph's and Mary's amazement and relief as they find the boy Jesus there. The last joyful mystery, then, is *Finding Jesus in the Temple*.

THE FIVE SORROWFUL MYSTERIES (46-50)

We move now to another section of the study, in front of a large picture window. The 46th location is the site of one of two low swiveling rockers. You note that a *garden* is growing from the seat of the first chair. But this is no happy garden scene. Jesus himself is kneeling there praying, sleeping apostles nearby. The first sorrowful mystery is the *Agony in the Garden*.

THE MYSTERIES OF THE ROSARY		
Location	**Image**	**Mystery**
		Joyful Mysteries
41. Study door	*A nun*	1st: Annunciation
42. Short bookcase	*Visitors'-info sign*	2nd: Visitation
43. Tall bookcase	*Nativity scene*	3rd: Nativity
44. Statue	*Presents*	4th: Presentation
45. Picture	*Jewish Temple*	5th: Finding Jesus in the Temple
		Sorrowful Mysteries
46. First chair	*Garden*	1st: Agony in the Garden
47. Tall lamp	*Pillar*	2nd: Scourging at the Pillar
48. Second chair	*Crown of thorns*	3rd: Crowning with Thorns
49. Foot rest	*Cross*	4th: Carrying of the Cross
50. Picture window	*Crucifix*	5th: Crucifixion

Next to the chair, at location 47, is a tall floor lamp. Can you see it as a *pillar* instead? The pillar presents a very sad sight, for this is the site of the *Scourging at the Pillar*, where Jesus felt the lash of the Roman soldiers. At location 48, on the other side of the pillar, is a matching swivel rocker, and on this one grows an even harsher garden, nothing but *thorns*. It reminds us of a further attempt to harm and humiliate Jesus, which we recall in the third sorrowful mystery, the *Crowning with Thorns*.

In front of the chairs is an ottoman foot rest (location 49). Resting on it is not a foot, but a *big stick*, the most famous stick and most recognizable symbol in all the world. It is, of course, the *Cross*. Imagine that Jesus picks up that stick, as he prepares for his most painful and greatest act. The fourth sorrowful mystery, then, is the *Carrying of the Cross*.

Imagine that when you turn to look out the picture window and into the front yard, at location 50, you see not that old familiar maple tree, but what would represent the most horrible of sites, if so much good did not come from it. The image you see is Jesus hanging upon that Cross. Can you imagine his mother and the apostles who loved him at this scene? The *Crucifixion* is the last sorrowful mystery, but glorious things are to come.

THE FIVE GLORIOUS MYSTERIES (51-55)

We know well that the last sorrowful mystery wasn't the end of the story of Jesus, but an incredible new beginning. Look at the globe on the pedestal in the corner on the study (location 51). As you look at this globe, the scene zooms in to the Holy Land, as if your eyes were the powerful lenses of a space satellite. You see an *empty cave*, with a boulder rolled to the side of its entrance. Jesus is not there. The first glorious mystery is the *Resurrection*.

Next to the globe, at location 52, is still another bookcase. As you look above it, you see the most amazing of sights. You see *Jesus rising up* into heaven, for the second glorious mystery is the *Ascension*.

There's a door at the other end of the study (location 53) and through that door descends *a beautiful dove*. It is Pentecost, and the dove is the symbol of the Holy Spirit. The third glorious mystery is the *Descent of the Holy Spirit*.

Next we move to location 54. Can you picture on the wall not one but *five paintings* depicting Mary's glorious *Assumption into Heaven*? (Please feel free to imagine a beaming Jesus too.) The last glorious mystery includes another crown, but not a crown of thorns. At location 55, on the back wall of the study, is one enormous portrait, and this one feature's Mary's crowning in heaven. The last glorious mystery of the Rosary is the *Crowning of the Blessed Virgin*.

THE FIVE LUMINOUS MYSTERIES (56-60)

The word *luminous* comes from the Latin word *lumen*, which means "light." A related Latin word for daylight is *luxor*. Perhaps the greatest simple line from the Latin version of the Old Testament is "*Fiat lux!*": "Let there be light!" Both Latin words also have connotations implying glory. These Luminous Mysteries focus on the brilliant light that Jesus shared with the world in the social ministry of his public life. Let's see where they are in the study.

I'm sitting right now in location 56 of our study, in front of the computer armoire that is location 57. In my mnemonic image I picture *a river flowing* all around me, and a very special scene is taking place in that river. John the Baptist is baptizing Jesus. The first luminous mystery is the *Baptism of Jesus*.

Next we come to the computer armoire (location 57). The real one is open right now, or I wouldn't be typing. But we'll imagine it's closed, and when we open it, we see a magnificent scene: an entire wedding feast. Of course, there has been a slight problem, for they have run out of wine. (Chapter 2 of John's Gospel tells us how Mary and Jesus intervened to solve that problem.) Can you picture this?

Location 58 is another bookshelf, to the side of the computer armoire, and we need another image of *Jesus* here, this time as a great *orator* proclaiming his message, parables, Beatitudes, and all, for the third luminous mystery is the *Proclamation of the Kingdom*.

Location 59 brings us to the last picture in our house. This one depicts Jesus on a high mountain where "*his face shone like the sun*

THE MYSTERIES OF THE ROSARY

Location	Image	Mystery
		Glorious Mysteries
51. Globe	*Radiant Jesus*	1st: Resurrection
52. Bookcase	*Jesus rising up*	2nd: Ascension
53. Doorway out	*Dove*	3rd: Descent of the Holy Spirit
54. Diplomas	*The Virgin Mary*	4th: Assumption of the Blessed Mary
55. Picture	*Jesus crowning Mary*	5th: Crowning of the Blessed Virgin
		Luminous Mysteries
56. Floor before armoire	*Flowing river*	1st: Baptism of Jesus
57. Armoire	*Wedding feast*	2nd: Wedding at Cana
58. Bookcase	*Jesus as crowned orator*	3rd: Proclamation of the Kingdom
59. Portrait	*Jesus changing appearance*	4th: Transfiguration
60. Closet door	*The Last Supper*	5th: Institution of the Eucharist

and his clothes became as white as the light" (Matt. 17:2). There are two figures next to him, Moses and Elijah. Just picture Jesus and these two great men, three luminous figures, bathed in a supernatural light of the *Transfiguration.*

Next you arrive at the 60th and last location of this mnemonic house. You open the closet door and see another incredible scene, for there is Jesus, surrounded by his disciples, and he says to them:

> "Take, eat; this is my body." And he took a cup, and when he had given thanks, he gave it to them, saying, "Drink of it, all of you; for this is my blood of the covenant, which is poured out for many for the forgiveness of sins" (Matt. 26:26-28).

The last of the Luminous Mysteries is the *Institution of the Eucharist*. I am writing in "The Year of the Eucharist." What better time to ponder this mystery?

And I hope that knowing these twenty mysteries by heart will facilitate our meditations upon them in the Rosary. It's also good practice to find these scenes in the Gospels and Church writings for a fuller appreciation of their context and details.

You'll recall that I promised to try to show how the subjects in the various chapters of this book are interrelated parts of the glorious whole that is our Faith. Here's another connection to ponder. We saw how the sacraments have been associated with the cardinal and theological virtues. Another way to derive benefit from meditating on the mysteries of the Rosary is to ponder various virtues and beatitudes that each scene displays. Then each day, we can go forth and try to live them. Here is a summary from *The New Roman Missal* by Father F. X. Lasance.

ROSARY MYSTERY	VIRTUE
Joyful Mysteries	
Annunciation	Humility
Visitation	Fraternal charity
Nativity	Spirit of poverty
Presentation	Obedience, purity
Jesus in the Temple	Love of Jesus, duty

Memorize the Faith!

ROSARY MYSTERY	VIRTUE
Sorrowful Mysteries	
Agony in the Garden	Fervor in prayer
Scourging at the Pillar	Penance, mortification of senses
Crowning with Thorns	Moral courage
Carrying of the Cross	Patience
Crucifixion	Self-sacrifice, forgiveness of injuries
Glorious Mysteries	
Resurrection	Faith
Ascension	Hope
Descent of Holy Spirit	Love and zeal for souls
Assumption	Filial devotion to Mary
Coronation of Mary	Perseverance

The summary from *The New Roman Missal* was written before the inclusion of the Luminous Mysteries. Which Christian virtues do those mysteries evoke in your mind?

ROSARY MYSTERY	VIRTUE
Luminous Mysteries	
Jesus' Baptism	________________
Wedding Feast at Cana	________________
Proclamation of the Gospel	________________
Transfiguration	________________
Institution of the Eucharist	________________

MEMORY MASTER TIPS AND FACTS

QUESTION 8

Weren't visual-imagery systems besides the method of loci used in medieval times?

One system popular during the Middle Ages, and still useful today, is to memorize information obtained from books by mentally picturing the actual page of text. This might be one reason some medieval texts were so carefully laid out and so artfully illustrated and decorated. It also argues for the value of attractive, carefully crafted books today.

Part 3

In My Father's House Are Many Mansions

Chapter 9

The Four Marks of the Church

"We believe in one, holy, catholic, and apostolic Church."

Nicene Creed

By now, you're probably becoming familiar with the rooms and their layouts, but please feel free to refer back to the pictures in the previous chapters as necessary. It takes some time and practice to learn the mnemonic rooms "by heart," but once you do, you'll be better able to appreciate their power fully. And in the chapters ahead we'll have plenty of practice!

Now that we've used the method of loci to build our house of faith, we'll see how those rooms can be remodeled, so to speak, allowing us to house a virtually limitless amount of new information. Are you familiar with the child's toy for drawing or writing with a plastic stylus and thin sheet covering a wax tablet? Just lift the sheet and the lines disappear, allowing for a brand-new message or picture. The method of loci works something like that toy. (Imagery-based mnemonic techniques have, indeed, been called "mental writing.") We can "lift the sheet" and write all kinds of new information on our memories. With the child's toy, the older impressions, although no longer visible on the sheet, do remain embedded in the wax. So too when we use our mental locations for new information: the older information is still embedded in the wax of our memory and can be recalled when we want.

So our next step is to "lift the sheet" on the six rooms we've used to house the Commandments, the capital sins, the virtues, the Beatitudes, the sacraments, and the Rosary mysteries — not to forget them, but rather, to inscribe additional important information. Jesus said his Father's house has many mansions. So too could the knowledge of our faith fill many stately mnemonic houses.

It's time, then, to grow in our mastery of the method of loci by applying our locations to new subjects. Much of the spiritual information we'll encounter next has been known within the Church for centuries, even millennia, although I imagine it might be news to many readers. But don't worry: it's all "good news," since it derives primarily from that fountain of good news, the Gospels.

Before we move on, note one important difference here. I laid out the rooms in our house with the specific materials from chapters 3 through 8 in mind. That's why the first room has ten loci, the second seven, and so on. But the house can be used as a framework to recall lists of any size (and, as you'll see later, of virtually limitless amounts of information). You simply have to match the number of loci in a room to the number of items you wish to remember. This chapter, for example, will introduce the Four Marks of the Church in the first four locations of the foyer. The next chapter will move along, still within the foyer, with the Four Last Things. The next chapter on the Five Precepts of the Church will start in the foyer and finish up in the living room. I think you'll see this poses no problem at all. But let's get busy now, to find out for sure.

The Four Marks of the Church

The four characteristics, or "marks," of the Church can be traced to the Gospels and epistles of the New Testament, and they're expressed most explicitly in the Nicene Creed. Although the words may roll off the tongue automatically during our Profession of Faith, every single word is rich with meaning and is there for a specific reason. This point is made most clearly by St. Thomas Aquinas in *The Aquinas Catechism*, wherein he explains fundamental Christian creeds and prayers literally word for word, showing what they mean and where they came from. The Apostles' Creed and the elaborated Nicene Creed are also covered in great depth in the *Catechism*. Make time to read up on it later. For now, let's get ready to build another mansion of memory.

Again we arrive at the front door of the house. From a short way down the street, you notice a huge mark of some sort on the front door. As you pull in the driveway, you see that a huge number *1* is painted on the door. The first mark of the Church is that it is *one*. Jesus and Paul spoke time and again of the essential unity and oneness of Christ's Church. Today, some five hundred years after the Reformation, there are tens of thousands of separated Christian denominations, which is, of course, a far cry from one. It would tax the ability of the world's greatest mnemonist to remember even a fraction of their names! Anyway, at the front door think *1*, for oneness is the first essential characteristic of Christ's Church.

On to the second location, the doormat, and it's a strange one indeed, for it's simply a huge slice of *Swiss cheese*. Why Swiss cheese? Because it's full of holes. Sorry, but *holy* is the second mark of the Church. Speaking seriously, the Church is undoubtedly made up of sinners, but it's also home to countless saints; moreover, it's the

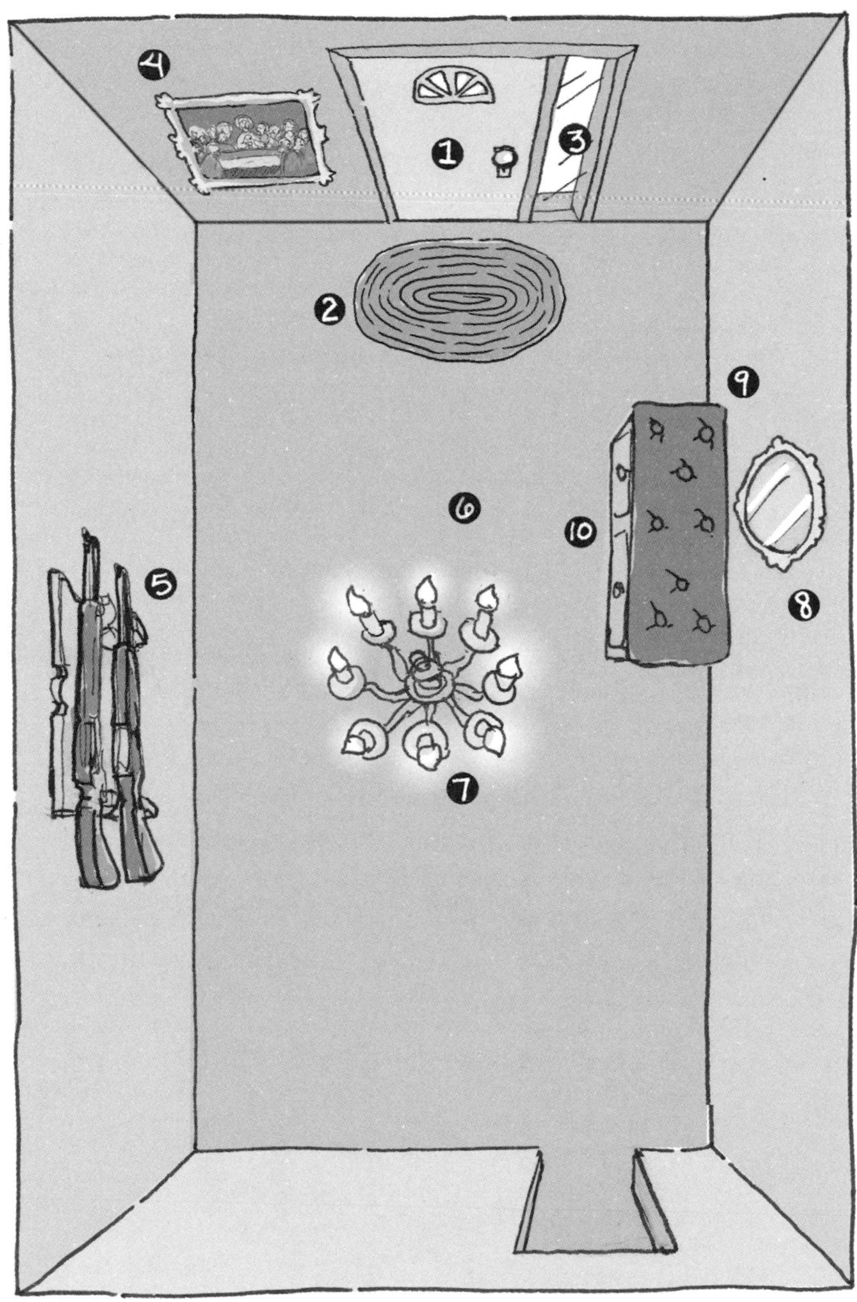

Foyer

Bride of Christ, and by virtue of its union with Christ, it has to be holy. Also, its function is to help make us holy — for example, through the sacraments (which I trust you can name by now; if not, take a quick peek back inside chapter 7's cathedral).

As we look out the glass panel (location 3) next to the front door, we see a *cat licking* its paws. The third mark, *catholic*, means "universal." It's clear in the Gospels that Christ intended the one unified Church to spread throughout the world, as indeed it has.

Location 4 is the portrait on the wall of the foyer and this portrait shows the *Last Supper*. Note well the Apostles in that portrait, because the last mark of the Church is that it is *apostolic*. The Church was based on the commission Christ gave to the Apostles, with Peter specifically designated as their leader. (We'll know them all by name by the time chapter 17 is finished.)

If you can recall the large 1 on the front door, the Swiss-cheese doormat, the cat licking in the front yard, and the portrait of the Apostles, then you know the Four Marks of the Church.

THE FOUR MARKS OF THE CHURCH

Location	**Image**	**Mark**
1. Front door	*1*	One
2. Doormat	*Swiss cheese*	Holy
3. Glass panel	*Cat licks*	Catholic
4. Portrait	*Last Supper*	Apostolic

MEMORY MASTER TIPS AND FACTS

QUESTION 9

How can I make my images more memorable?

First, don't worry about making them perfect. Begin by seeing what associations naturally come to your mind when creating concrete images for abstract concepts. And here's a tip from a medieval memory master: St. Albert the Great, echoing an ancient Roman tome on the art of memory, advises us to make memory images "as striking as possible," to picture them "doing something" and having "exceptional beauty or singular ugliness." The key idea, then, is exaggeration. Make the images big, bold, fantastic, and memorable — and have some fun with them. You'll be training your imagination, as well as your memory.

Chapter 10

The Four Last Things

"The Christian who unites his own death to that of Jesus views it as a step towards him and an entrance into everlasting life."

Catechism of the Catholic Church, 1020

Our focus has been on principles of Christian living. But as St. Thomas Aquinas often reminds us, proper actions are determined by their ends. We often think of an end as something that comes last, and this is correct in one sense — in the case of the Last Things, they certainly do come "last," at the end of our lives and at the end of the world. But there's another sense in which an end is an organizing and motivating principle. The Four Last Things should also be considered in this sense: to remind us Christians of the highest and final end deriving from our hope and faith — namely, to enjoy eternal bliss in the presence of God. That end should be the strongest of motivators guiding us toward charitable decisions in this life. Being mindful of death, judgment, heaven, and hell can be a *beginning*: a beginning of good choices.

The first Last Thing brings us to the fifth location in our tour of the mnemonic house — namely, the *gun rack* in the foyer. It should not be too hard to link the gun rack with *death*. We might also picture the image of the *Grim Reaper*, setting aside his sickle and pulling a gun from the rack. Next, in the center of the foyer, you spy a huge glowing figure holding a large wooden mallet and dressed in a *judge's robes*. This will remind us of *judgment*. Moving to the seventh location, the chandelier, you look up at it and see a portal into *heaven* itself. Make this image as bright and vibrant as you can imagine it. The next image should be as disconcerting as the last was uplifting, for when you glance at the mirror you see the *flames of hell*. Imagine the frame beginning to darken and crack from the heat.

If you can recall the Grim Reaper at the gun rack, the glowing judge in the center of the foyer, the portal to heaven through the chandelier, and the flames of hell in the mirror, then you know the names of the Four Last Things. You can turn to paragraphs 1020-1060 of the *Catechism of the Catholic Church* for an explication of their meaning.

THE FOUR LAST THINGS

Location	Image	Thing
5. Gun rack	*Grim Reaper*	Death
6. Center of foyer	*Glowing judge*	Judgment
7. Chandelier	*Portal to heaven*	Heaven
8. Mirror	*Flames of hell*	Hell

MEMORY MASTER TIPS AND FACTS

Question 10

Why can't we remember events from our infancy?

The word *infancy* derives from the Latin adjective *infans*, which means "unable to speak." As important as images are to memory, theorists such as Lev Vygotsky (introduced in chapter 29 of this book) have also stressed the vital role of human speech and language to the development of all higher human thinking capacities, including reasoning and memory. It takes a few years before nature (including the brain) and nurture (including the speech we hear from others) produce the capacity for speech and memory. So I don't advise trying these systems with your newborn!

Chapter 11

The Five Precepts of the Church

"The precepts of the Church are set in the context of a moral life bound to and nourished by liturgical life."

Catechism of the Catholic Church, 2041

The *Catechism of the Catholic Church* posits five precepts "to guarantee to the faithful the very necessary minimum in the spirit of prayer and moral effort, in the growth in love of God and neighbor" (2041). These represent the bare minimum for active Church membership and for spiritual growth. Let's look at them before we begin:

1. You shall attend Mass on Sundays and holy days of obligation and rest from servile labor.
2. You shall confess your sins at least once a year.
3. You shall receive the sacrament of the Eucharist at least during the Easter season.
4. You shall observe the days of fasting and abstinence established by the Church.
5. You shall help to provide for the needs of the Church.

The first precept brings us to the ninth location in the foyer, the bench under the mirror. Can you imagine a beautiful small-scale model of *your own church* sitting on that bench? Better yet, imagine a radiant *sunrise* behind it. This will help us remember the need to *attend Mass every Sunday*. Next, you pull open one of the small drawers in the bench, but you shut it very quickly, once you see a small penitent and confessor inside. This is our reminder of the need for *yearly confession*.

For the third precept we move to the eleventh location, the center of the living room. Here again we find good *St. Thomas* holding the Eucharist aloft, saying, "*You Christ*," as he did at the altar in chapter 7. This time, however, you also notice that St. Thomas is surrounded by huge *Easter baskets*. This will remind us of the need to *receive the Eucharist, especially around Easter*.

You spy the fourth precept through location 12, the picture window. In the backyard are several *sprinters* crouching at their blocks. Their goal is to run *fast*. Their purpose for us is to remind us of *fasting and abstinence*. (It doesn't hurt that St. Paul has compared the Christian life to running a race; 1 Cor. 9:24; Heb. 12:1).

THE FIVE PRECEPTS OF THE CHURCH

Locations	**Images**	**Precepts**
9. Bench	*Your church/sunrise*	Mass on Sundays
10. Drawer	*Penitent/confessor*	Yearly confession
11. Center of living room	*"You Christ"/ Easter egg*	Eucharist during Easter season
12. Picture window	*Fast runners*	Fasting and abstinence
13. Sofa	*Shingles/money*	Providing Church needs

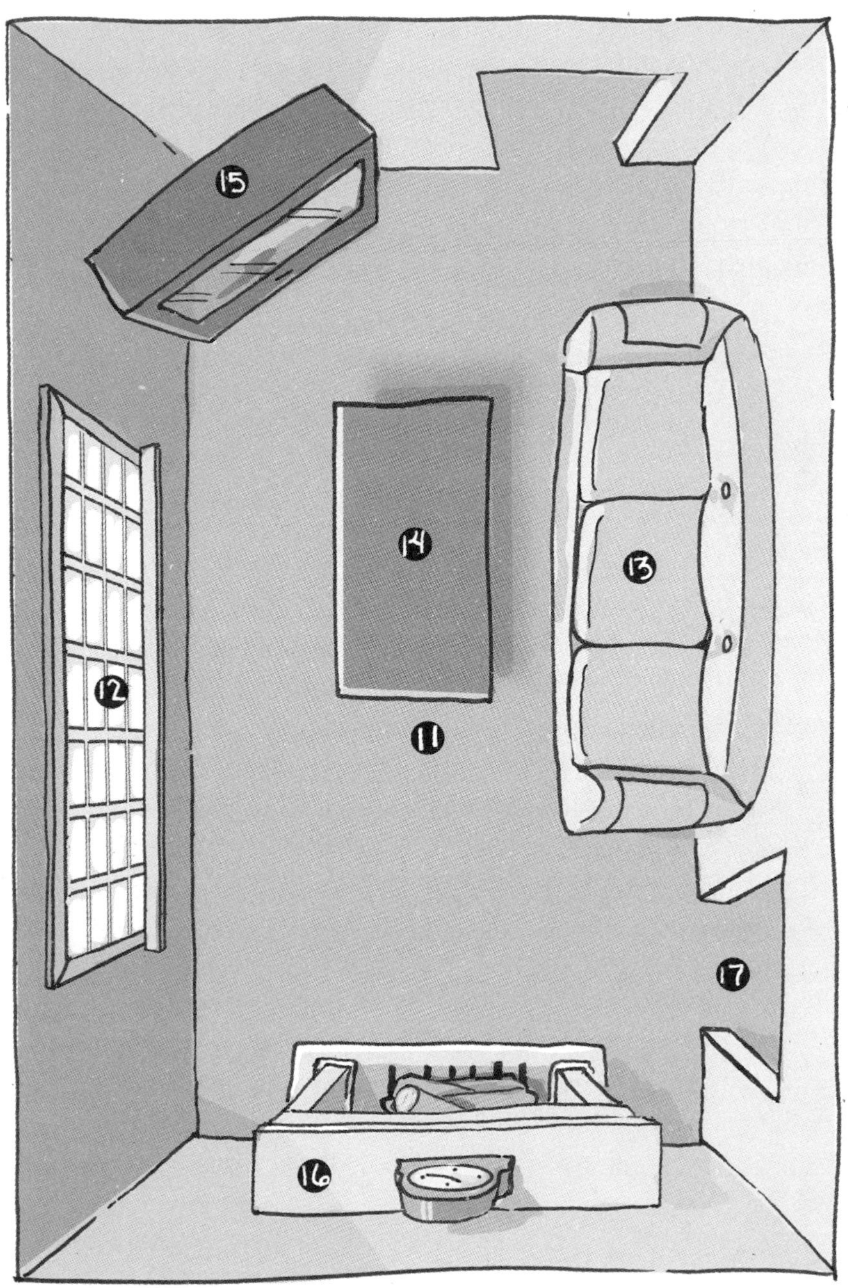

Living Room

On now to the thirteenth location and fifth and last precept. We are now at the living-room sofa. Ask yourself, what does your church need? A new roof? Money to keep its school going? Whatever it needs, place those needs on the sofa, and be sure to check under the cushions, too. (Perhaps it won't be the first time you've found some money there!) The fifth precept, of course, compels us to attend to the needs of the Church.

MEMORY MASTER TIPS AND FACTS

QUESTION 11

What is short-term memory?

Short-term memory refers to the human capacity to hold on to a limited amount of information (usually about seven items for adults) in conscious awareness for a limited amount of time. Its capacity develops as we age. Below is a summary from research on one of the basic measures of short-term memory called *digit span* (the maximum number of digits a person is able to repeat back in the same order after hearing them once). Bear in mind that these are average findings and memory capacities can vary a little from person to person.

Age	Maximum Digit Span
2	2
5	4
10	6
12	7
70	6

Chapter 12

The Six Sins Against the Holy Spirit

"There are no limits to the mercy of God, but anyone who deliberately refuses to accept his mercy by repenting, rejects the forgiveness of his sins and the salvation offered by the Holy Spirit."

Catechism of the Catholic Church, 1864

This is serious business. Some critics of Christianity have said that Jesus' remarks on the unforgivable nature of blasphemy against the Holy Spirit (Matt. 12:32; Mark 3:29; Luke 12:10) have caused untold misery to Christians throughout the ages who have wondered whether they might have at some point inadvertently committed such a sin and forfeited their salvation. Well, it isn't as simple as that.

Blasphemy of the Holy Spirit doesn't happen inadvertently or accidentally; in fact, it takes considerable malevolent intention. God's mercy is so great that we must actively work against it to forfeit it completely. The Catholic Church has elaborated considerably on this important topic, and in just a minute we'll look at the six sins it has defined.

Let me just note in passing that a wonderful little novel relevant to this theme (and to the Last Things as well) is C. S. Lewis's fantasy *The Great Divorce* (the divorce being not between a human couple, but the great divide between heaven and hell). Here a busload of people from hell take a day trip to heaven. Lewis portrays well how completely and resolutely those folks down below have chosen their own destination by rejecting God's mercy.

Anyway, on to the sins. The first sin against the Holy Spirit will be found on the coffee table in the living room. Watch out! A bowling ball has rolled down that table and knocked over a few remaining bowling pins, thus making *the spare*. The first sin, as you might have guessed, is *despair*. It means the complete abandonment of hope in one's salvation through God's goodness.

Next, at the fifteenth location, the big-screen television, you see the picture *zooming* in on your favorite *priest*. Priest and zooms will remind us of *presume*, and *presumption of God's mercy* is the second sin. The *Catechism* (2092) tells us that we may presume either by overconfidence in our own ability to earn salvation without God's help, or by presuming of God that he will grant us our salvation without any effort or merit on our part.

Next, we move on to the fireplace and the third sin against the Holy Spirit. We notice a bright place in the fireplace, but no logs. After looking very closely, we see that, oddly enough, it's only a *puny tooth* putting forth the flames. The third sin, then, is *impugning the known truth*. This means to willfully and actively attack, contradict, distort, or falsify spiritual matter we know to be true.

The last site of the living room is the doorway leading into the dining room. Here, in the seventeenth location, resides the fourth sin against the Holy Spirit, and it's a doozy. Here we see a green, raging, muscular *Incredible Hulk*. He's wrestling with a spirit, and he's growing smaller. This sin is the most virulent species of the capital sin of envy, the *envy of another's spiritual good*. The opposite of charity, it begrudges another his hope of happiness and salvation. The Hulk is shrinking because this sin, although grave, is so small and petty.

On now to the dining-room entranceway, location 18, and the fifth sin against the Holy Spirit. Here we find, riding on a mule, a doctor on his way to deliver a baby. Why do we find this? Because the specialist in delivering babies is an *obstetrician*, and mules are known for being stubborn or *obstinate*. They represent *obstinacy in sin*. It means stubbornly refusing the power and gifts of the Holy Spirit. This might include willful ignorance of virtue and refusal to fight against our own vices.

Finally, we come to the head of the table (location 19) and the last of the sins against the Holy Spirit. Here we see a large *funnel in* which *pens* and *ants* are being poured onto the chair. Final impenitence, you see, is difficult to visualize, but we'll do our best with *funnel*, *in*, *pens*, and *ants*. (You might want to work a little longer on this one.) Final impenitence is most profoundly grave and sad. It is man's final and explicit rejection of God and his mercy. It

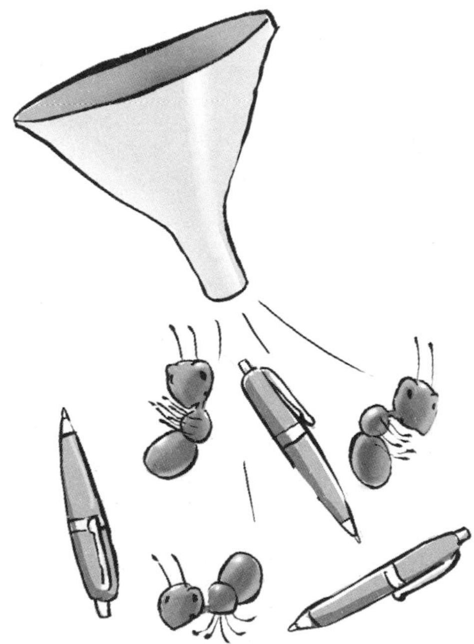

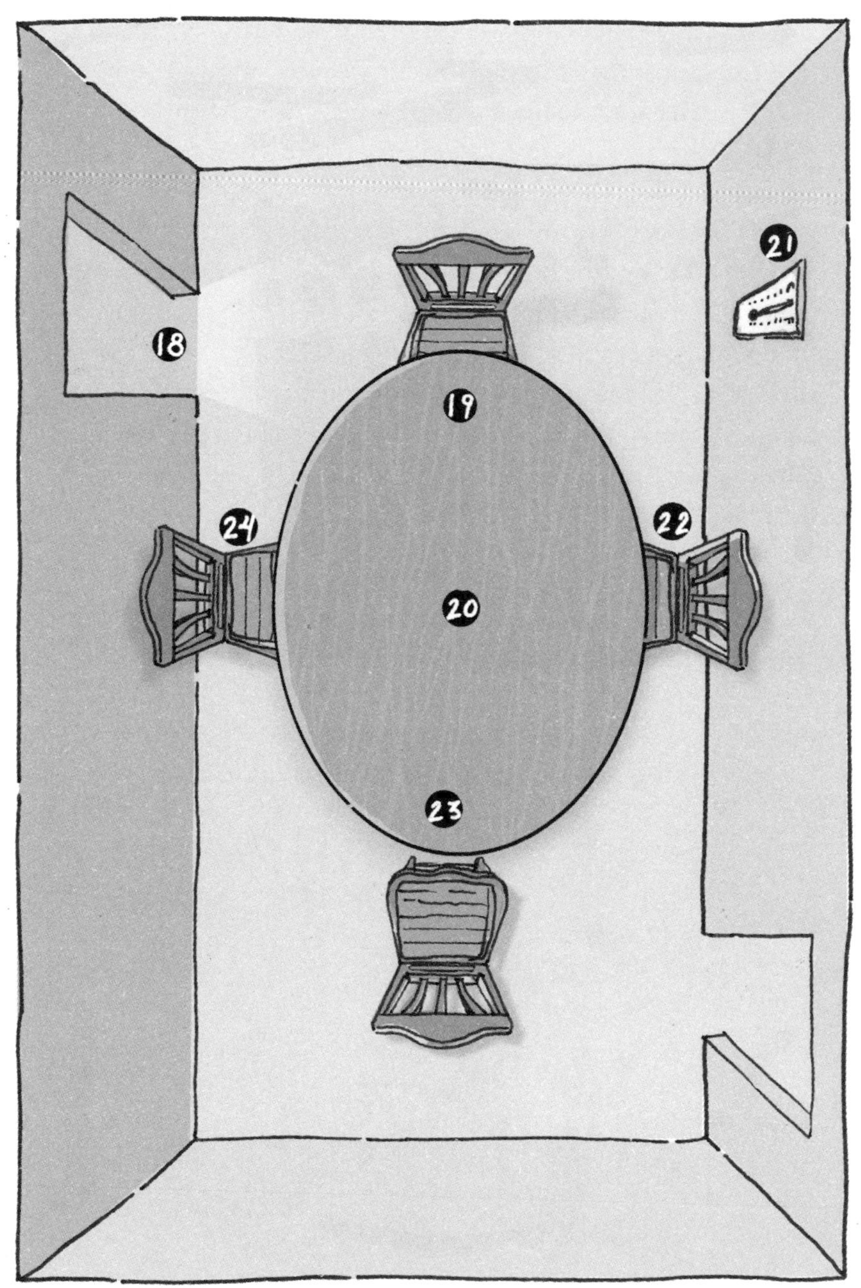

Dining Room

is an unwillingness to be contrite or to seek out forgiveness, to be without regret, shame, or remorse for our sins.

There they are. To learn more, you might want to examine the Bible verses cited above and paragraphs 1864, 2091, and 2092 in the *Catechism*.

THE SIX SINS AGAINST THE HOLY SPIRIT

Locations	**Images**	**Sins**
14. Coffee table	*Bowling spare*	Despair
15. Big-screen TV	*Priest zooms*	Presumption
16. Fireplace	*Puny tooth*	Impugning truth
17. Living-room doorway	*Hulk wrestling spirit*	Spiritual envy
18. Dining-room doorway	*Obstetrician riding mule*	Obstinacy in sin
19. Head of table	*Funnel, in, pens, ants*	Final impenitence

MEMORY MASTER TIPS AND FACTS

QUESTION 12

What is long-term memory?

Long-term memory refers to the nearly limitless capacity of virtually permanent memory storage. The goal of mnemonic techniques is to help us register information in our long-term memories, so we'll be able to use it when we need it later on.

By the way, when information is drawn from your long-term memory, it appears again for a while in your short-term memory. Who wrote the four Gospels? If, before reading this, you're already thinking "Matthew, Mark, Luke, and John," then you've recalled this information from your long-term memory, and the evangelists are now also in your short-term or "working memory" for a while. (Question 13 will address "working memory.")

Chapter 13

The Seven Gifts of the Holy Spirit

"The seven gifts of the Holy Spirit are wisdom, understanding, counsel, fortitude, knowledge, piety, and fear of the Lord."

Catechism of the Catholic Church, 1831

Drawing first from Isaiah 11:2-3, and building on insights from great Church Fathers (and even Aristotle), St. Thomas elaborates on seven gifts of the Holy Spirit in the *Summa Theologica* (I-II, 68). He considers eight questions about their nature, including how they relate to the virtues. In a nutshell, he explains in depth how they're gifts of God that provide higher perfection of the virtues. The *Catechism* discusses the gifts in paragraphs 1266, 1299, and 1831. It notes that these gifts of the Holy Spirit belonged most fully to Christ, but they're given to sustain the moral life of all Christians. In the sacrament of Confirmation, the bishop's prayer over the recipient confirms and invokes the outpouring of all seven gifts of the Holy Spirit.

Let's put on our thinking (and remembering) caps now and get down to business. We've arrived at the twentieth location in our mnemonic house, the center of the dining-room table. We're pleasantly surprised to see that the rest of the dining room is filled with gift-wrapped packages for us, especially when we learn that these gifts are from the Holy Spirit!

Let's unwrap them, one by one. This dining-room table is big. When you climb on top to unwrap the gift at the center of the table, you realize that you're standing under an amazing chandelier that looks at first to be made of crystal. Soon you realize that the sparkling radiance is coming not from crystals, but from ideas. The gift you're *standing under* is *understanding*. The next location (21) is the wall thermometer, and it is, as you might expect, being licked by a cow dressed in silk (well, maybe you didn't expect that), since *cow in silk* sounds enough like *counsel* to remind us of the second gift.

Next, to the seat on the right, location 22. Here we find a giant *wisdom tooth*, roots and all, since the third gift is *wisdom*. On now to the foot of the table (23) and another strange sight. There you see a small mountain with a little man slipping down its side, crying out, "There's no ledge!" *No ledge* should remind us of *knowledge*, the fourth gift.

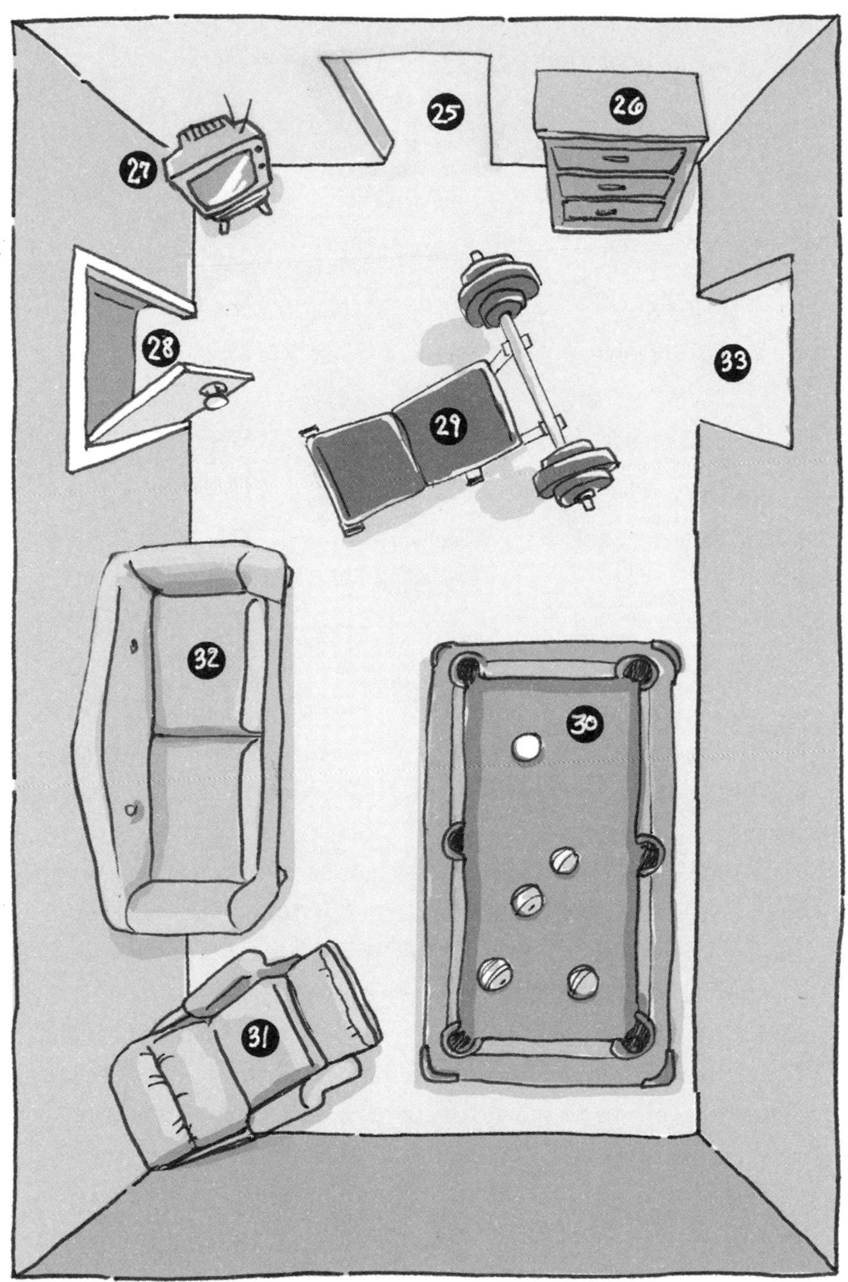

Family Room

THE SEVEN GIFTS OF THE HOLY SPIRIT		
Location	**Image**	**Gift**
20. Center of table	*Standing under chandelier*	Understanding
21. Thermometer	*Cow in silk*	Counsel
22. Seat on right	*Wisdom tooth*	Wisdom
23. Foot of table	*Mountain: "No ledge!"*	Knowledge
24. Seat on left	*Fresh-baked pie*	Piety
25. Door to family room	*Child's fort*	Fortitude
26. Dresser	*Woman praying/ trembling*	Fear of the Lord

St. Thomas notes that the first four gifts (understanding, counsel, wisdom, knowledge) belong to reason, and the last three (piety, fortitude, and fear of the Lord) to appetite. Let's take a look at those.

We next arrive at location 24, the seat on the left. Be careful before you sit! Look at the seat of the chair and the steam coming off your favorite fresh-baked *pie* (blackberry, pecan — you decide). The fifth gift of the Holy Spirit is *piety*.

It's time to visit the family room now to pick up the sixth gift, but blocking the door is a massive child's model of a *fort*. We used a fort in the chapter on the virtues to represent fortitude, and there's also a form of *fortitude* that's a gift from the Holy Spirit.

Last, but not least, is the family-room dresser at location 26. Here you see a *woman kneeling devoutly in prayer*, and you notice she is *trembling*. The last gift of the Holy Spirit is a proper *fear of the Lord*.

MEMORY MASTER TIPS AND FACTS

QUESTION 13

What is working memory?

Working memory in the general sense refers to the fact that short-term memory is an active process. For example, if you were going to call someone and needed to remember the seven digits of a phone number that someone just told you, you might work on them as you walked toward the phone by repeating them to yourself. If you wanted to move the numbers to long-term memory to remember them for good, you might repeat them more often and with more attention, perhaps grouping the numbers and paying close attention to their sounds. (Stay tuned for more on working memory in another later chapter.)

Chapter 14

The Seven Spiritual Works of Mercy

"The works of mercy are charitable actions by which we come to the aid of our neighbor in his spiritual and bodily necessities."

Catechism of the Catholic Church, 2447

In the epistle of St. James we read that "faith without works is barren" (James 2:20). Okay, then, exactly what kinds of "works" does our faith bid us do? For centuries the Church has spoken of seven spiritual works of mercy and seven corporal works of mercy, culled from the scriptures. These acts by which we minister to our neighbor's spiritual needs are addressed briefly in the *Catechism* (2447) and in depth by St. Thomas (*ST*, II-II, 32) under the heading of "Almsdeeds." This list is slightly wordy, so let's look at the Seven Spiritual Works of Mercy up front:

1. Instructing the ignorant
2. Counseling the doubtful
3. Comforting the sorrowful
4. Reproving the sinner
5. Forgiving injuries
6. Bearing wrongs patiently
7. Praying for the living and the dead

Now, back to our house. Location 27 is the small television set in the family room, and who but *St. Thomas Aquinas* should be on the air, behind a podium, *instructing those ignorant of the Faith* out in TV land. The next location is the closet, and here we find that *cow in silk* again! The second spiritual work of mercy is to advise, or *counsel, the doubtful.* We find location 29, the weight-lifting bench, covered like a bed with a *comforter*, and lying there all alone, a person is *crying*. As Christians, we are impelled to *comfort the sorrowful* as we share God's mercy.

On now to the pool table, and there is your own (real or imagined) son, enjoying a leisurely game. You recall, however, that he had promised to mow the neighbor's lawn. You gently get him *moving*, since the fourth spiritual act of mercy is to *reprove sinners.*

THE SEVEN SPIRITUAL WORKS OF MERCY

Location	Image	Spiritual Work
27. Television	*St. Thomas instructing*	Instructing the ignorant
28. Closet	*Cow in silk*	Counseling the doubtful
29. Weight bench	*Comforter/ crying person*	Comforting the sorrowful
30. Pool table	*Son playing/ not mowing*	Reproving the sinner
31. Recliner	*Bandaged man*	Forgiving injuries
32. Couch	*Bear bearing lash*	Bearing wrongs patiently
33. Doorway out	*People praying over casket*	Praying for the living and the dead

We go next to the recliner (location 31), except it looks more like a hospital bed. The *man* lying there has his foot in the air and is *bandaged* from head to toe. Our job (the fifth spiritual work of mercy), when injured physically or spiritually, is to forgive those who hurt us.

At location 32, we arrive at the family-room couch, and oddly enough, there's that bear again (the one from bearing persecution and reviling in the chapter on the Beatitudes). Here, let's imagine the *bear patiently putting up with mistreatment from a trainer's lash*, because the sixth spiritual work of mercy is *bearing wrongs patiently*.

The seventh and last of the spiritual works of mercy is what we see when we open the family-room door: a group of *people praying* over a casket. The last spiritual work of mercy, then, is to *pray for the living and the dead*.

MEMORY MASTER TIPS AND FACTS

QUESTION 14

What about encoding, storage, and retrieval?

Human cognition, as seen through what modern psychologists call an "information processing model," includes capacities, or "structures," like short-term memory and long-term memory. It also includes "processes" that describe how information moves back and forth between various cognitive structures. For memory, the basic processes are encoding (getting information into the system), storage (holding it), and retrieval (pulling it back out). Surely you can see how mnemonic systems are involved in encoding information. It's easy to see how our unusual mnemonic images serve as codes to represent the material we really seek to remember.

The method of loci also makes for a very organized system of storage — literally "a place for everything and everything in its place" — as well as a built-in retrieval system, since the places cue or trigger recollection of the images.

Chapter 15

The Seven Corporal Works of Mercy

"Now the love of our neighbor requires that not only should we be our neighbor's well-wishers, but also his well-doers. . . ."

Summa Theologica, II-II, 32, 5

Man, of course, is a being of body as well as spirit, and so our task now is to register in our minds the works of the body. The corporal (bodily) works of mercy address the important physical needs of our fellowman. St. Thomas points out that the corporal works, like the spiritual works, are actually "act[s] of charity through the medium of mercy" (II-II, 32, 1).

As we did with their spiritual counterparts, let's look at the list of the Seven Corporal Works of Mercy before re-entering the house.

1. Feeding the hungry
2. Giving drink to the thirsty
3. Clothing the naked
4. Harboring the harborless
5. Visiting the sick
6. Ransoming the captive
7. Burying the dead

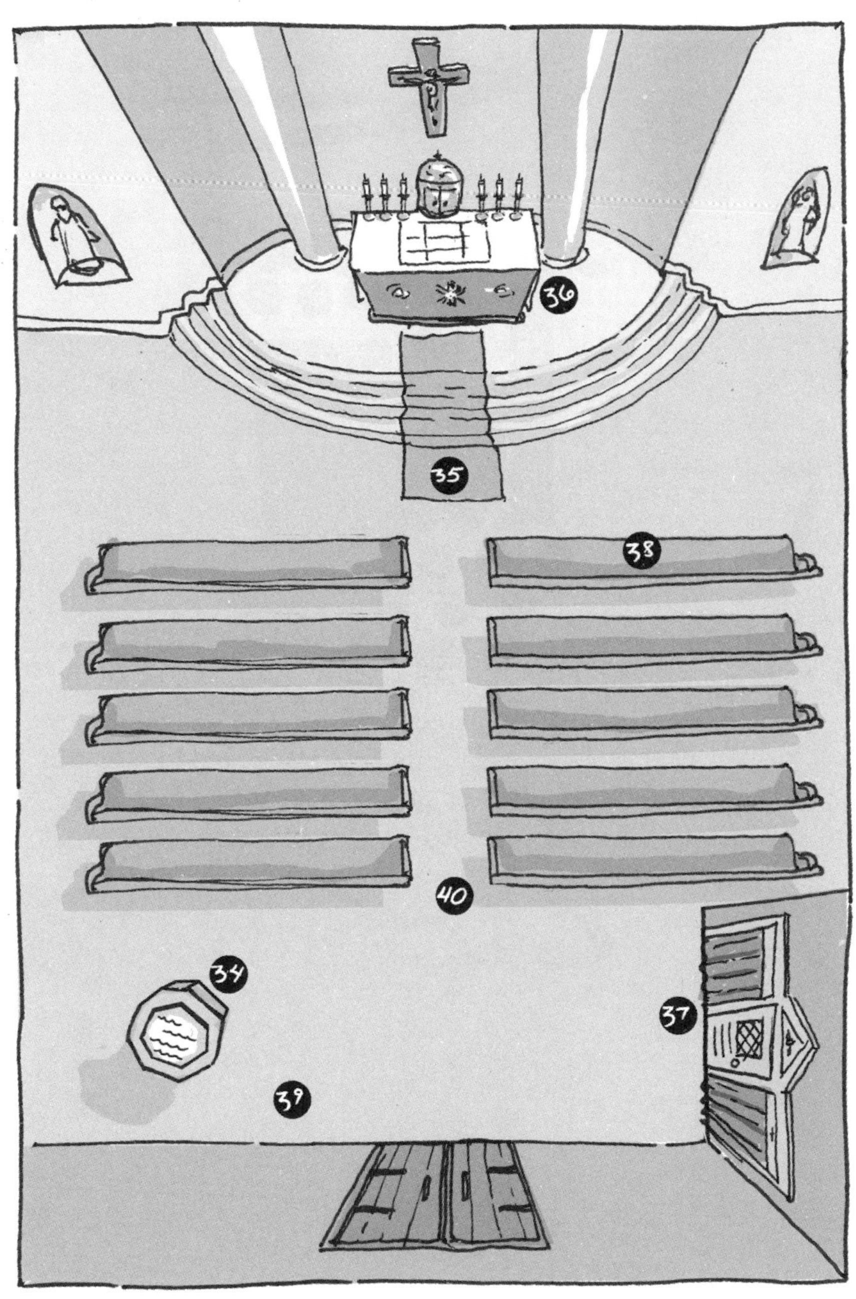

Cathedral

Since these works are corporal, we'll find them easy to transform into memorable images. Let's now enter the mnemonic cathedral. There, at location 34, the baptismal font, we see *a priest giving a loaf of bread to a starving person*. At the center in the front of the first row of pews (35), imagine a *thirsty man* being quenched by *water and wine* from a chalice.

At the altar (36), imagine *a fellow parishioner placing a new robe on a poor, naked person*, whose tattered rags have fallen from his body. On to the confessional (37), which, you notice, is surrounded by *water and small boats*. The fourth corporal work is to *harbor the harborless* (in more modern language, perhaps, to house the homeless).

Next we go to the front of the right bank of pews, and there we spy another *bandaged person*. The fifth corporal work is to *visit the*

THE SEVEN CORPORAL WORKS OF MERCY

Location	**Image**	**Corporal Work**
34. Baptismal font	*Priest feeds hungry*	Feeding the hungry
35. Center front	*Wine and water*	Giving drink to the thirsty
36. Altar	*Parishioner with clothes*	Clothing the naked
37. Confessional	*Water and boat*	Harboring the harborless
38. Front pew right	*Bandaged person*	Visiting the sick
39. Back of church	*Tied, gagged person*	Ransoming captives
40. Start of center aisle	*Casket*	Burying the dead

sick. At the back of the church (39), we see that *someone is tied and gagged* on that very chair, and our job is to *ransom the captive*. Fortunately, this is not something most of us do every day in today's world, but note again how it involves the willingness to take action to relieve another's bodily distress.

Last, at the start of the center aisle (40), we encounter the last corporal work of mercy. There lies a *casket*, and our job will be to respect the deceased and accompany him to his *burial*. You may wonder why it could be a work of mercy to do something for a person who is already dead. Hear St. Thomas on the respect due to the very body of the deceased:

> Nevertheless, it does concern the deceased what is done with his body: both that he may live in memory of man whose respect he forfeits if he remain without a burial, and as regards a man's fondness for his own body while he was yet living, a fondness which kindly persons should imitate after his death (II-II, 32, 2).

MEMORY MASTER TIPS AND FACTS

QUESTION 15

Can you remember these? ✈ ❐ ◆ ⌧ ● ⚠ ❖ ■ ❍

Take just a minute to memorize them, and then close your eyes and see how many you can recall. Okay, how did you do? But more important, *what did you do* to remember them?

This little exercise demonstrates the difference between verbal and visual memory. Verbal memory is memory of things expressed in language, and visual memory is memory of things we perceive through our vision, such as shapes and colors. In this book, we have called forth visual images to assist our verbal memories. But in this particular exercise, I'm pretty sure you used your verbal abilities to help you remember visual information. Didn't you say to yourself things like, "an airplane, white square, black diamond, black circle"? Verbal memory is most closely connected with activity on the left side of the brain in most people (even left-handers), and visual memory is most closely connected with activity on the right side of the brain. Artificial memory techniques rev up *both* sides!

Chapter 16

Ten Holy Days of Obligation in the Latin Rite of the Catholic Church

"On Sundays and other days of obligation the faithful are bound to participate in the Mass."

Catechism of the Catholic Church, 2192

Christians are obliged to pay homage to God on Sunday, of course. We haven't forgotten the Third Commandment, after all. But on the Church's liturgical calendar can also be found ten special feast days, on which we are obliged to attend Mass.[3] Here are special days of celebration, respect, and remembrance that enrich our lives in every yearly cycle — another manifestation of the fullness of the Catholic Church. Let's learn these holy days.

We're back to the study, the last room in our mnemonic house, and half of its locations will be ample to store the Holy Days of Obligation, providing enough remaining locations to squeeze in the twelve Apostles too in the next chapter (if a few don't mind

[3] These are the ten "universal" holy days, but not all are celebrated as days of obligation for Mass in all parts of the world. Also, for practical purposes, such as the travel limitations of priests in some areas, when some of these holy days fall on a Saturday or a Monday, attendance at Mass isn't obligatory.

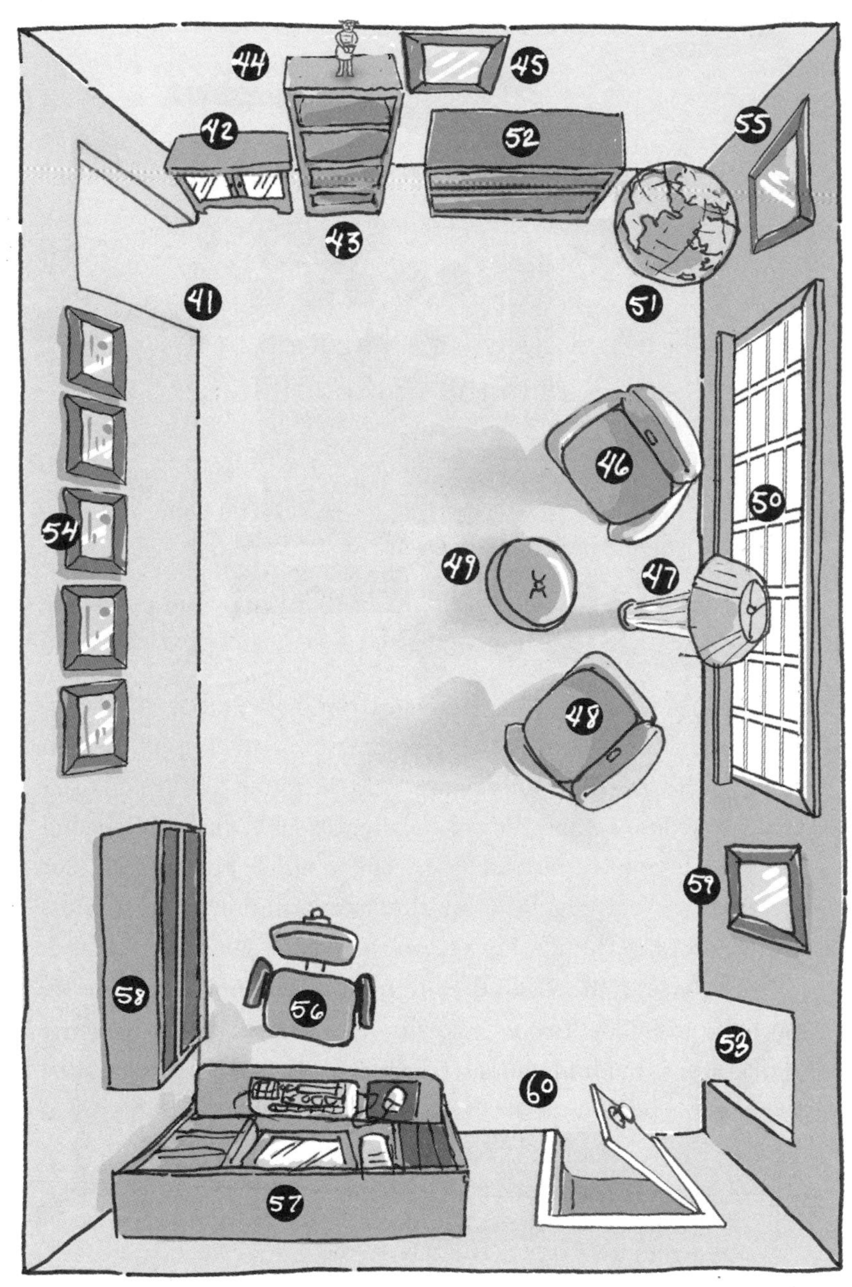

Study

sharing a spot). Location 41 is the doorway to the study. Picture the *infant Jesus in the manger* just inside the door, since the holy day is the first *Christmas*. Moving along to the small bookshelf (42) we see the *Magi*, three wise Gentiles witnessing the manifestation of God in Christ. It's the *Epiphany*. (If the Magi alone don't call the word *epiphany* to mind, try imagining that you're watching them riding in on a funny hippo. Get it? "*Hippo funny*" sounds as much like *epiphany* as anything that comes to my mind at the moment.)

At the site of the tall bookshelf (43) is *Jesus rising into the air* — the feast of his *Ascension* into heaven. Imagine next, that the statue on the shelf (44) is *Jesus Christ himself*, his *bloody wounds* apparent. This is the feast of *Corpus Christi*, the feast of the *Body and Blood of Christ*. Above and to the right of this statue is a portrait (45) of *Mary, the Mother of God*, holding Christ's body, as in Michelangelo's *Pietà*.

Now let's move to the next section of the study, where we'll store the remaining holy days. The 46th location is the first swivel chair, and there lies a *most beautiful baby girl*, the newborn Mary. This holy day is the feast of her *Immaculate Conception*. When you turn on the lamp (47), an amazing scene transpires. *Mary herself*, a

TEN HOLY DAYS OF OBLIGATION IN THE LATIN RITE OF THE CATHOLIC CHURCH

Location	Image	Holy Day
41. Study door	*Infant Jesus*	Christmas (December 25)
42. Small bookcase	*Magi/hippo*	Epiphany (January 6)
43. Tall bookcase	*Jesus rising*	Ascension (forty days after Easter)
44. Statue	*Jesus' body*	Body and Blood of Christ*
45. Picture	*Mary/Jesus*	Mary, Mother of God (January 1)
46. First chair	*Baby Mary*	Immaculate Conception (December 8)
47. Floor lamp	*Mary rising*	Assumption of Mary (August 15)
48. Second chair	*Tired carpenter*	Feast of St. Joseph (March 19)
49. Foot rest	*Peter/Paul*	Feast of Peter and Paul (June 29)
50. Picture window	*Souls coming*	All Saints' Day (November 1)

*This feast's date varies, depending on the date of Easter.

woman now, *rises toward heaven*, body and soul. This is the feast of the *Assumption*.

At location 48, the other swivel chair, picture a *carpenter* from days gone by in dusty sandals and cloak. He is wiping his brow, his day's work done, knowing he has provided for his young family. The carpenter, of course, is *St. Joseph*, and his day is our eighth holy feast.

At the ottoman footstool (49) imagine *two more men sharing a seat*. You've imagined these great men before. One was a rock, and the other a bit like a rolling stone. Both men built Christ's Church, and both men died in Rome. Of course, they are *Peter and Paul*, and they are jointly celebrated on this, our ninth holy day.

Finally, it's dark outside on a dark autumn evening. The doorbell rings. You look out the picture window and what do you see? Not ghoulish trick-or-treaters, but a *gathering of thousands of great souls*, the blessed saints of the Church throughout the ages, for our last Holy Day of Obligation is the feast of *All Saints*. Make sure you get to Mass!

MEMORY MASTER TIPS AND FACTS

QUESTION 16

What metaphor did Aristotle use for memory?

In his book *On Memory*, Aristotle likens memories to perceptions that have been stamped in the mind, like impressions made with a seal. Consider the seal of a signet ring impressed on a wax tablet. Aristotle likens our minds to the wax tablet and notes that the minds of some, such as those of the very young or the very old, might be either too soft or too hard to receive impressions very well.

Chapter 17

The Twelve Apostles

"Follow me, and I will make you fishers of men."

Matthew 4:19

Think back now to the portrait of the foyer on this second tour through the mnemonic house. It contained a famous painting that represented for us the fourth mark of the Church. That's right: it was the Last Supper and the mark was "apostolic." Here now, we present that original group of twelve men chosen by Jesus to build his Church and proclaim his Word to the world. The Apostles are listed in the Bible in texts including Matthew 10:2, Mark 3:16, Luke 6:14, and Acts 1:13, and I'm following the order presented by St. Matthew. We'll fit these great men into the second half of our little mnemonic study, but I'll also tell you where their images actually exist in one of the most glorious locations on earth.

Inside the basilica of St. John Lateran in Rome are beautiful, enormous statues of all twelve Apostles. If you should ever happen to visit that basilica, I wouldn't mind in the least if you mnemonically relocated the Apostles there. Now back to the study.

Location 51 is the globe on the pedestal. Let's have our imaginary space satellite zoom in to the Holy Land and picture a *fisherman sitting on a rock*. This again is *Peter* (also known as Simon), the first of the twelve told by Jesus that they would become "fishers of men." He would later become the Rock upon which the Church would be built. Next is another bookcase (52), and here sits Simon Peter's brother *drawing* in the sand with a stick, for *Andrew* is his name. Passing by the door (53) is a *man playing games*, this to remind you that his name is *James*. Checking out the diplomas on the wall (54) is another brother, beginning to *yawn*, for he's James's brother *John*. (It's interesting to consider that these Apostles needed no diplomas and no special learning to fulfill their roles. God's grace works great deeds through ordinary souls.) And, oh yes, feel free to imagine a blazing bolt of lightning, and a powerful clap of thunder between the door and diplomas, since Mark tells us that Jesus called James and John *Boanerges* which means the "Sons of Thunder." Next is another portrait, this one (55) on the west wall. Strangely enough, the picture begins to *flip* back and forth to remind us of the apostle's name, *Philip*.

Location 56 brings us to the space in front of the computer armoire, where I sit clicking away at the keyboard. I see an apostle motioning me toward him, and I answer, "*Bart, I'll follow you.*" For the sixth apostle is Bartholomew. Looking into the computer armoire (57), and at the screen, who should we see there but *St. Matthew himself*, dictating to us this list of Apostles as found in his Gospel, since Matthew is the next apostle. Location 58 is another bookcase, and sitting upon it is a man who tells you he *doubts* it will hold him. Initially less willing to believe what his eyes had not seen than the St. Thomas who is guiding us, this is his namesake, *St. Thomas the Apostle*. On the wall is a portrait (59), and painted there are *two games*, to remind us that there are *two Jameses*. At the south door was James the son of Zebedee, and this is *James the son of Alphaeus*.

Now, *one* location, but *three* apostles remain. Three in One should pose no problems for Christians! In this case we will see some of the flexibility of the method of loci and get the slightest

THE TWELVE APOSTLES

Locations	**Images**	**Apostles**
51. Globe	*Fisherman on rock*	Simon Peter
52. Bookcase	*Brother and drawing*	Andrew
53. Doorway out	*Games*	James (son of Zebedee)
54. Diplomas	*Man yawns*	John
55. Picture	*Picture flips*	Philip
56. Floor before armoire	*"Bart, I'll follow you."*	Bartholomew
57. Armoire	*St. Matthew giving list*	Matthew
58. Bookcase	*Thomas doubts it will hold*	Thomas
59. Portrait	*Two games*	James (son of Alphaeus)
60. Closet	*Gladius sword*	Thaddeus
	"Simon Says" game	Simon
	Man flees in chariot	Judas Iscariot

taste of its full potential. Sure, we could imagine additional loci, but who says there can be only one image per location? In fact, I'll show later on, especially in the chapter on Church history, that each location can hold a wealth of information. Each image we place in a location in this book can be merely a starting point for more.

On to the last apostles now, though. Imagine that when we open the closet door (60) we find three men, a little bit cramped. The first holds a short Roman sword, called a *gladius* (from which we get the word *gladiator*) to remind us that the tenth apostle's name is *Thaddeus*. And weren't we just talking about games again with James? Let's imagine the second man is telling the other two some things to do. Yes, they're playing "*Simon Says*," because the apostle is *Simon*. Last, and, yes, in a crucial way least, is a guilty man fleeing in a *chariot*, for he is the betrayer of Jesus, *Judas Iscariot*. Of course, since there's not much room for a chariot in the closet, you might want to imagine the chariot bursting through the back wall for greater effect.

MEMORY MASTER TIPS AND FACTS

QUESTION 17

What's the difference between memory and recollection (or reminiscence)?

Aristotle, St. Albert, and St. Thomas emphasized the distinction between memory and recollection (also translated as *reminiscence*). We share with lower animals the capacity to hold on to impressions. Hence, Aristotle, St. Albert, and St. Thomas placed *memory* in the "sensitive," or animal, part of the soul. *Recollection*, however, consists of purposefully searching the contents of our memories to recall something we've previously learned, and among animals only rational man has this power.

Chapter 18

The Twelve Fruits of the Holy Spirit

"The fruits of the Spirit are perfections that the Holy Spirit forms in us as the first fruits of eternal glory. The tradition of the Church lists twelve of them: charity, joy, peace, patience, kindness, goodness, generosity, gentleness, faithfulness, modesty, self-control, chastity."

Catechism of the Catholic Church, 1832

Building on the words of St. Paul in Galatians 5:22-23, St. Thomas provides explanation and insight regarding the Twelve Fruits of the Holy Spirit in the *Summa* (I-II, 70). To put it in a nutshell (or perhaps an orange peel), Thomas points out that "the fruits are any virtuous deeds in which one delights . . ." (I-II, 70, 2). As fruit is produced by the tree, so too are good works the produce of man. As material fruits please and refresh us, so too do spiritual fruits, "with a holy and genuine delight." The *gifts* make us receptive to the inspiration of God, so that we may bear (and enjoy) the *fruits*. If you'd care to delve deeper into the nature of the fruits, including their relationship to the virtues, gifts, and Beatitudes, go again to Thomas.

At this point, let me ask you, have our two tours through the house of memory borne fruit for you, not only in terms of the *content* we've memorized, but in terms of the *method*? Are you, dear reader, acquiring the ability to build mnemonic loci and images yourself? Let's put it to the test in this chapter. For the Twelve Fruits of the Holy Spirit, you're welcome to use any of the rooms of the house to store any information of your choosing. You can also feel free to create locations of your own. So, in this chapter I'll leave it all up to you. Here are the fruits: charity, joy, peace, patience, kindness, goodness, generosity, gentleness, faithfulness, modesty, self-control, and chastity.

Place the fruits in a room or two of the mnemonic house, or better yet, why not add on a couple of rooms from your own home? Are you sitting in one of them now? If not, just imagine one. How about your bedroom? Can you think of ten locations in your bedroom and ten more in another bedroom? (Creating mnemonic

THE TWELVE FRUITS OF THE HOLY SPIRIT

Location	Image	Fruit
________	________	Charity
________	________	Joy
________	________	Peace
________	________	Patience
________	________	Kindness
________	________	Goodness
________	________	Generosity
________	________	Gentleness
________	________	Faithfulness
________	________	Modesty
________	________	Self-control
________	________	Chastity

rooms in groups of ten is a very nice way to proceed. It makes it very easy to keep track of the numbers. Our rooms have locations of varying numbers only because I originally designed them to house the lists in part 2 of this book.) Since the contents in this chapter are "fruits," they could even be imagined in the produce department of your grocery store, or in your refrigerator and cupboards, if you'd like to experiment.

When you have your room and locations, move on to the fruits and the images. Just ask yourself, "What concrete image does this word first call to my mind?" Nothing right away? Then ask yourself, "What else does it sound like?" The pronunciation of *charity*, for example, made me think of "chair with tea," as we saw in chapter 5 on the seven virtues. Now it occurs to me that "cherry tea," or perhaps, for a golfer, a "cherry tee" would be other possibilities. Does *charity* call to your mind any other concrete image?

In forming your images, make them stand out in your mind's eye. We tend to forget the ordinary, but hold on to the unusual. Make your images large. Make them silly, if you like. Make them dynamic and active. But don't worry about making them perfect. Sometimes the very effort involved in forming a less-than-perfect mnemonic will help you remember the content all the more.

Let's recall again St. Thomas's four rules, from chapter 2. Since you started reading this book you've taken care of the *concentration* and the *repetition*. Now I'm leaving the *organization* (locations) to you, as well as the *unwonted images*.

MEMORY MASTER TIPS AND FACTS

QUESTION 18

Have there been other popular memory metaphors?

Many ancient writers (such as St. Augustine and St. Jerome) have likened memories to "treasures" of the mind. Medievals often depicted and described "chains" of memory, emphasizing how they can be linked with techniques like the method of loci. Some modern psychologists are fond of describing memory systems as "cognitive tools"; after all, they can help us hammer home, lock in, and build up all kinds of knowledge. We couldn't have built this house without them!

Chapter 19

The Fourteen Stations of the Cross

"The Council of Trent emphasizes the unique character of Christ's sacrifice as 'the source of eternal salvation' and teaches that 'his most holy Passion on the wood of the Cross merited justification for us. And the Church venerates his Cross as it sings: "Hail, O Cross, our only hope."' "

Catechism of the Catholic Church, 617

The Stations of the Cross present incomparable scenes for contemplation, not just during Lent, but at any time of the year. The stations are typically represented with beautiful images on the walls of Catholic churches. Each station presents an image so vivid and so powerful that I see no need for substituting other images for them.

The role of imagination here will instead be to elaborate on these gripping scenes in your mind's eye. In fact, you might want to involve all of your senses. Can you hear the crowd, feel their jostling, smell the odors, taste the dust in the air? Can you imagine the events from Christ's perspective? What is he seeing and feeling? Make your images of each station as vivid as possible. It will help you remember them, and it will help you appreciate the magnitude of Christ's sacrifice.

THE FOURTEEN STATIONS OF THE CROSS

Location	Image	Station
________	________	1st: Jesus is condemned to die.
________	________	2nd: Jesus takes up the Cross.
________	________	3rd: Jesus falls the first time.
________	________	4th: Jesus meets his mother.
________	________	5th: Simon helps Jesus carry his Cross.
________	________	6th: Veronica wipes the face of Jesus.
________	________	7th: Jesus falls the second time.
________	________	8th: Jesus meets the women of Jerusalem.
________	________	9th: Jesus falls the third time.
________	________	10th: Jesus is stripped of his garments.
________	________	11th: Jesus is nailed to the Cross.
________	________	12th: Jesus dies on the Cross.
________	________	13th: Jesus is taken down from the Cross.
________	________	14th: Jesus is laid in the tomb.

To allow you further practice with the creation of loci, I'll leave them up to you. You could use the rooms of the house if you like. Another possibility is to place your mnemonic images on the pictures or reliefs of the Stations on the walls of your own church, right where they'll come in most handy. For more information on the Stations, there are books and several sites on the Internet that address them in detail. The Stations are a tradition of the Faith well worth looking into and contemplating regularly.

All right. We've covered a great deal of important information in part 3 of this book. Let's take a break before returning to face some very important challenges in part 4. There we'll put our mnemonic powers to the test with some conceptually difficult (e.g., the proofs of God's existence) and mnemonically challenging (e.g., the forty-six books of the Old Testament) material. But you'll receive plenty of guidance, and I hope you'll be glad that you stopped by the house once more.

MEMORY MASTER TIPS AND FACTS

QUESTION 19

Who were the ancient men with "divine" memories?

In ancient writings on artificial memory, several authors, including Cicero, the historian Pliny the Elder, and even St. Augustine, mentioned people with extraordinary memory powers. To give but a few of many extant examples, Pliny wrote that the Persian King Cyrus knew the names of all the men in his army and Lucius Scipio knew the names of all the Roman people. St. Augustine wrote of a friend who could recite the poetry of Virgil — backward. Cicero wrote of a man named Metrodorus who could recite people's statements back to them in their own words. He described the memory of Metrodorus (who was considered a charlatan by some) as "almost divine."

Part 4

Grow in Grace and in Knowledge of Our Lord

Chapter 20

Five Proofs of the Existence of God

"I answer that, The existence of God can be proved in five ways."

St. Thomas Aquinas, *Summa Theologica*, I, 2

One of the things for which St. Thomas Aquinas is most famous is his discussion of five proofs of the existence of God, in the first part of the *Summa Theologica.* Although he doesn't spend much space on them — just a couple of pages — his proofs have generated thousands of pages of commentary over the years. Thomas uses these five proofs to establish through reason alone the most basic thing we can know about God: that he must exist.

Building on this base, he explores many more fascinating aspects of the knowledge that we can obtain about God through the use of reason. For example, have you ever considered whether God could create a stone so heavy that even he couldn't lift it, or whether God could erase something that has already happened, making it so that it never did happen?

Thomas gives answers, but it's beyond our scope to provide them here. Please "go to Thomas" if you're intrigued. (The proofs are also addressed in a very accessible and straightforward manner in *Aquinas's Shorter Summa.*)

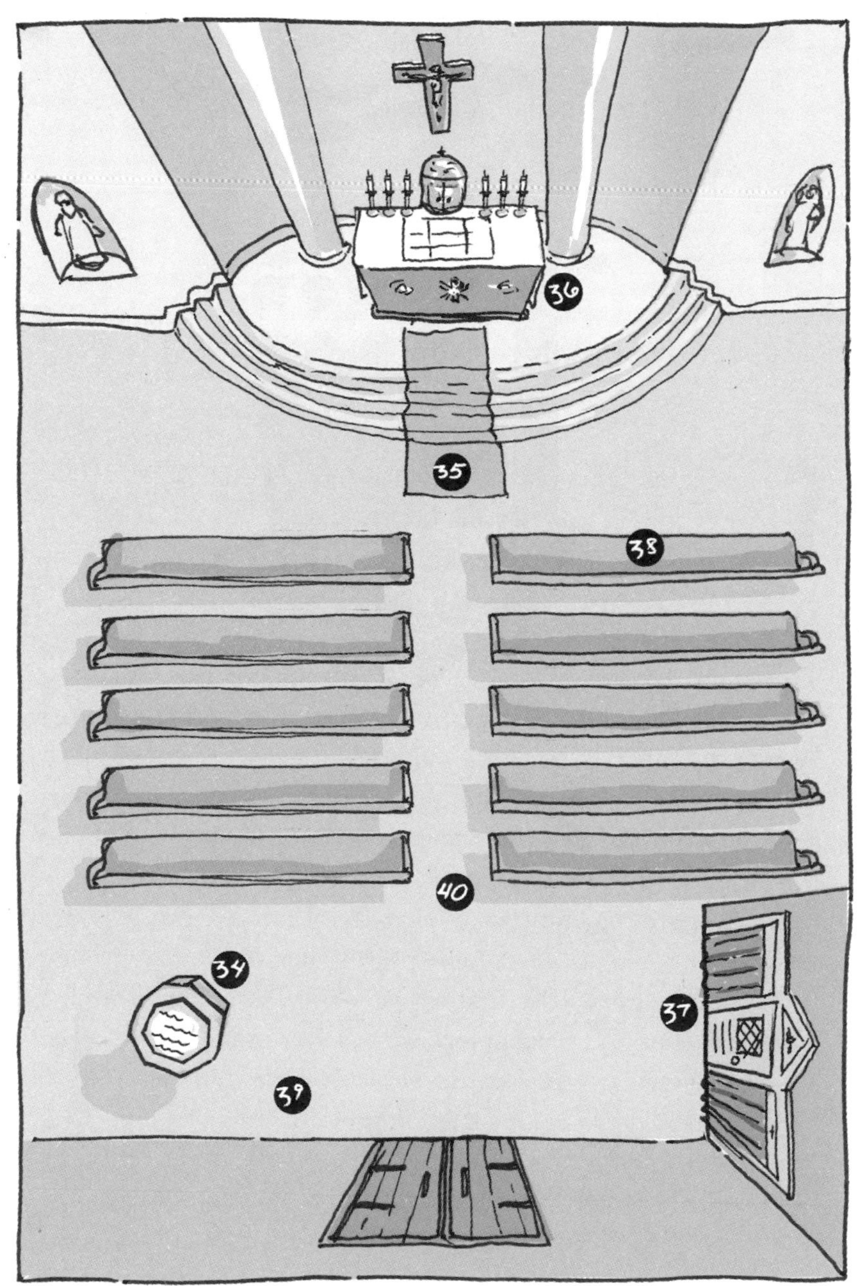

Cathedral

The five proofs can be quite abstract and can challenge the understanding. I won't address them in great depth here, but I recommend that you read the first part of the *Summa Theologica* (second question, third article), as well as commentaries from later thinkers (e.g., twentieth-century French Thomist philosopher Etienne Gilson's *The Christian Philosophy of St. Thomas Aquinas.*) Because the proofs are so abstract, I'll help out here by providing some concrete mnemonic images. And because the subject matter of the proofs is so exalted, I'll use the mnemonic cathedral to store it.

Imagine that when you enter the cathedral, the baptismal font is completely blocked by an enormous, unmovable *moving van*. The first proof for the existence of God, you see, is based on the fact that everything in the material world is in *motion*, and that to have set it all in motion initially requires the existence of an "*Unmoved Mover,*" which we call God.

Next, imagine that between the front pews is a *fisherman* casting his line toward the baptismal font. At the end of his line, instead of a hook, is a pair of *enormous claws. Fishing claws* will remind us of the argument from *Efficient Cause*. This proof, bearing some relationship to the first one, is based on the impossibility of an infinite regress of causes and effects; that is, something had to be the first, uncaused cause: God.

Moving along, you see something unusual on the altar. It's a bees' nest. You look a little too closely and suffer a *nest of scary bee stings*. Although this is a bit farfetched, I bet it will remind you of the proof from *Necessary Being*. This third proof is based on the distinction between the contingent and the necessary; or, that which depends on something else for its existence, and that which can exist on its own. It proves not that God might exist, but that he truly *must*.

The fourth location within the cathedral is the confessional. Imagine that you dart into the confessional to avoid those bees at the altar. The light outside the door, however, doesn't just indicate that someone is in there. It shines more brightly the more bee stings a person has. You see, it indicates the *degrees of bee stings*. This recalls the fourth proof: *Degrees of Being*. This proof sails into the deepest of philosophical waters, and I'm just going to hug the coastline. I'll simply note that it identifies God as the ultimate perfection of being.

Last, but not least, you peep out of the confessional at the front of the right bank of pews. That fisherman is getting ready to go home, but first he must find all of the claws he has been using as hooks. If we can remember his self-admonition *to "find all claws,"* surely we'll remember the proof by *Final Cause*.

This fifth argument sails into the heady waters of Aristotelean and Thomistic "teleology" (the view that natural processes operate for a purpose, goal, or end). A final cause is an ultimate end, and ends are the reasons, the "that for the sake of which" something occurs.

Please permit me to offer a homely example. Why are my fingers pressing these keys right now? Because I have a goal: I hope

ST. THOMAS'S FIVE PROOFS OF THE EXISTENCE OF GOD

Location	Image	Proof from/by
34. Baptismal font	*Moving van*	Motion
35. Center front	*Fishing claws*	Efficient Cause
36. Altar	*Nest of scary bee stings*	Necessary Being
37. Confessional	*Degrees of bee stings*	Degrees of Being
38. Front pew right	*Find all claws*	Final Cause

that readers like you will someday read these words. Without this goal, the keys just sit there. But why do I have such a goal? Partly because of my human nature, which includes the capacity to imagine the possible outcomes of my actions. And why do I have a human nature? Those who reject the concept of final cause would say that the answer is *chance* (which really isn't saying much).

Thomas would say that human nature (and all of nature, for that matter) is part of God's plan. Not only in man's actions, but in every action, from the movement of the heavenly bodies to the growth of plants, regular patterns of lawlike activity can be observed. Such regularity is not produced by chance. Randomness, rather, is chance's bedfellow.

Thomas argued that all of nature moves toward ends. Since this includes beings without intelligence, their movement must be directed by an intelligence, "as the arrow is shot to its mark by the archer. Therefore, some intelligent being exists by whom all natural things are directed to their end; and this being we call God" (*ST*, I, 3). All of creation, then, is like an arrow of God, the ultimate archer, guiding nature toward the targets he has selected (and created).

MEMORY MASTER TIPS AND FACTS

QUESTION 20

Why have artificial memory techniques been so neglected in modern times?

There are probably many reasons, including the widespread availability of printed materials. But perhaps, ironically, some of the reports of people with "almost divine" memories have actually tarnished the reputation of artificial memory. Some people might question the usefulness of reciting poetry backward, or memorizing *pi* to thousands of places past the decimal point. But the great medieval Doctors of the Church saw artificial memory as a useful aid to living a virtuous life, and that's why we're applying it to subject matter that's more than "almost divine"!

Chapter 21

The Forty-Six Books of the Old Testament

"The Old Testament is an indispensable part of Sacred Scripture. Its books are divinely inspired and retain a permanent value, for the Old Covenant has never been revoked."

Catechism of the Catholic Church, 121

By now, you have gone through the rooms of the mnemonic house at least two times. I hope you're feeling at home with them, but again, please feel free to refer back to the pictures in part 2 as necessary, until you know them by memory, forward and backward. In this chapter we'll encounter the greatest mnemonic feat we've attempted so far by tackling a topic of great importance for all Christians, and perhaps especially for Catholics.

Our subject matter now turns to inspired books of the scriptures themselves. The Bible is divided into two mains parts, of course. The Old Testament contains the sacred Hebrew scriptures from before the birth of Christ. The New Testament contains those sacred books that tell the story of the Old Testament's fulfillment, in the life, death, and Resurrection of Christ and in the early activities of the Church he established on earth. A greater familiarity with both old and new will increase our knowledge of God, his revelation of himself in history, and the salvific work of Christ and his Church.

Even so, it appears that many Catholics suffer from a Bible deficiency. Sure, we hear it read every Sunday at Mass (and some devout souls hear it daily), and we have a beautiful edition at home (perhaps several), but if we were to create an honest visual image of our Bible, would it be a little dusty? The Bible is the original written cornerstone of our faith and thought; its themes and language have shaped the course of the entire Western world (and are not unknown in the East). Our Protestant brethren love it and know it well, and even the modern secularist cannot call himself educated without a knowledge of the Bible's contents. Yet we Catholics are too often guilty of a degree of ignorance where Scripture is concerned.

Help dispel that ignorance by learning the names of all the books of the Bible. I think you'll find that memorizing them, including those of the Old Testament, can serve as a helpful aid in its study, if only for the fact that it will enable you to search its contents easily when tracking down a story or a verse. There will be no need to look at the table of contents when the order of all the books is neatly stored in your own head! Also, once you have the books in their mnemonic locations, you can embellish them by adding additional information, including some of your favorite verses. (That will come in the chapters ahead.)

Because there are so many books in the Old Testament (forty-six in the full complement of the Catholic edition), I'd like to address briefly the issue of memory capacity before diving into them.

The normal limits of a person's short-term memory (what he can keep in active awareness at one point in time) is approximately seven meaningful pieces of information, such as the seven digits of a telephone number. A psychological researcher of the 1950s called seven the "magic number" of short-term memory. Some psychologists talk about "seven, plus or minus two" to indicate that for healthy adults, the range of five to nine meaningful chunks of information will cover the limits for just about everybody. What we'll strive to do in this chapter is to memorize *forty-six* chunks of meaningful information in a relatively short time (although we will strive to move them into the almost limitless realms of long-term memory). This may prove a bit taxing for those of us born without the mighty intellect of Thomas Aquinas (even though we'll be using the system that he helped bring to us). Bearing this difficulty in mind, I will group the Old Testament books according to our mnemonic rooms, none of which exceed ten locations. Learning just one room at a time is a fine accomplishment, and that's what I recommend. For those who find they're capable of learning them all in one sitting, I welcome you to give it a try. For some, although not all people, this is definitely possible. Let's see what we can do.

Let's return to the front door of the house that leads us to the foyer. Is there a need for a mnemonic image for *Genesis*, the first book of the Bible? Probably not for most of us, especially if we're aware that the word itself stands for "beginnings" or "origins." Nonetheless, just in case, I'll provide an image. Imagine you open the front door and see someone you know named Jennifer, as well as her sister — "*Jen and sis*" (*Genesis*). Can you picture them? (Let's say they've come over to learn the books of the Bible, since that would be quite in keeping with our purposes.) You then notice that the doormat is boldly embroidered with the word "*Exit*," a rather straightforward reminder for the book of *Exodus*. Looking out through the familiar glass panel, you notice a giant pair of *Levi's* blue jeans lying out in the front yard. *Levi* reminds us of *Leviticus*. The picture on the wall is, oddly enough, full of nothing but *Numbers*. Maybe the artist was fascinated with the number *pi* and there it is: 3.1415 . . . carried out to thousands of digits. (As painful — and perhaps as useless — as it might sound, there actually are memory experts who have memorized *pi* to thousands of

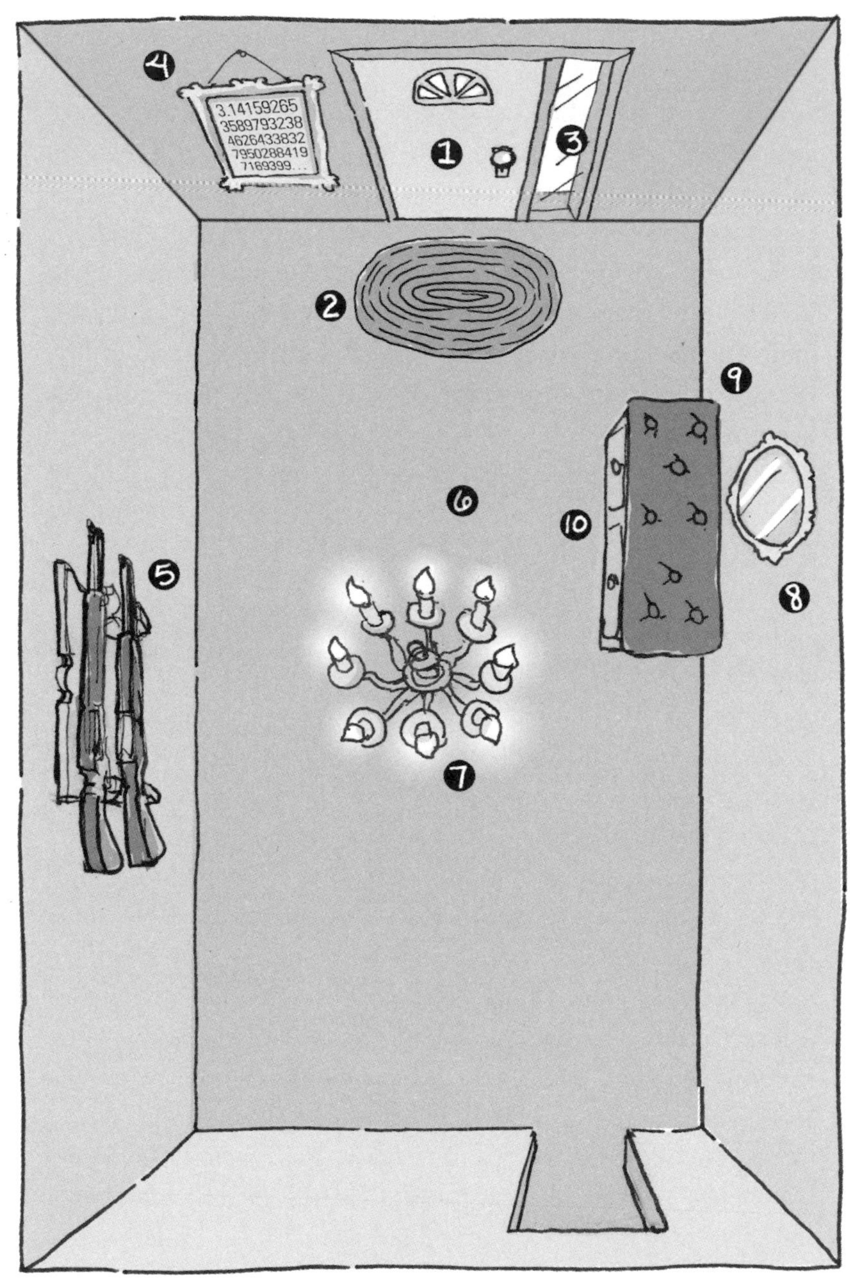
3.14159265
3589793238
4626433832
7950288419
7169399...
1
2
3
4
5
6
7
8
9
10

Foyer

places past the decimal point! But we have more important business at hand.) Okay, to recap, so far we have *Jen and sis: Genesis; Levi: Leviticus; Exit: Exodus;* and *Numbers:* well, *Numbers*. Let's carry on.

Next, you notice that the gun rack is full, not of guns, but of *telescopes*. You conclude they must be there to "*do astronomy*" (*Deuteronomy*). In the center of the foyer stands a man named *Joshua*. Do you know a Joshua? If so, place him right there. If you're familiar with the biblical Joshua himself, you could also use him as an image. One of the more memorable songs from my Catholic grade-school years is the one that goes "Joshua fit the battle of Jericho, and the walls came tumblin' down." Picture Joshua blowing a trumpet to blow down some walls if that will help you lock in the next image. Next is the chandelier, and looking overhead, you notice that instead of candles, the chandelier is composed of little glowing statues of *judges*, black robes and all, with their gavels raised and emitting beams of light. These little judges can surely help us recall the big book of *Judges*. Next you look in the mirror on the wall. You see not your own reflection, but the reflection of baseball legend *Babe Ruth*. Now, if you actually know a Ruth, or are familiar with a drawing of the biblical Ruth, you may certainly feel free to substitute another image. Just be sure you use a Ruth, since we need to recall the book of *Ruth*. We conclude with the last two locations of the foyer with a pair of twins, both named *Sam*. Imagine a Sam you might know, or even *Uncle Sam* — that is, a pair of them. One Sam is sitting on the bench under the mirror, and his twin is opening one of the drawers of the bench. Our Sams represent the two books of Samuel, referred to as *1* and *2 Samuel*.

If you practice and repeat these images in your mind's eye until you have them memorized, the foyer will have given you the first ten books of the Bible, in order (*Genesis*, *Exodus*, *Leviticus*, *Numbers*, *Deuteronomy*, *Joshua*, *Judges*, *Ruth*, *1* and *2 Samuel*).

THE BOOKS OF THE OLD TESTAMENT

Location	Image	Book
1. Front door	*Jen and sis*	Genesis
2. Doormat	*"EXIT" sign*	Exodus
3. Glass panel	*Levi's jeans*	Leviticus
4. Portrait	*Numbers*	Numbers
5. Gun rack	*Telescopes: Do astronomy*	Deuteronomy
6. Center of foyer	*Joshua/tumbling walls*	Joshua
7. Chandelier	*Little judges*	Judges
8. Mirror	*Babe Ruth*	Ruth
9. Bench	*Uncle Sam*	1 Samuel
10. Drawers	*Uncle Sam's twin*	2 Samuel

Let's move into the living room to memorize the next seven books.

In the center of the living room is a giant white chess piece, the *king*, to be exact, and it's facing the picture window looking out into the backyard, where a massive black chess piece — yes, *the other king* — is staring back at it. Our next two books, then, are *1* and *2 Kings*. At this point, you notice a bit of a chill. Why? Because the sofa is covered with *icicles*. In fact, a little frozen bridge connects the sofa to the coffee table, also covered with *icicles*. Two locations with icicles give us *1* and *2 Chronicles*. (Granted, *icicles* is a bit of a stretch for *chronicles*. Use two books from C. S. Lewis's *Chronicles of Narnia* instead, if you prefer, but either set of images should get the job done if you work at it.) Moving now to the site of the big-screen television, you see the image of a *zebra*. If you

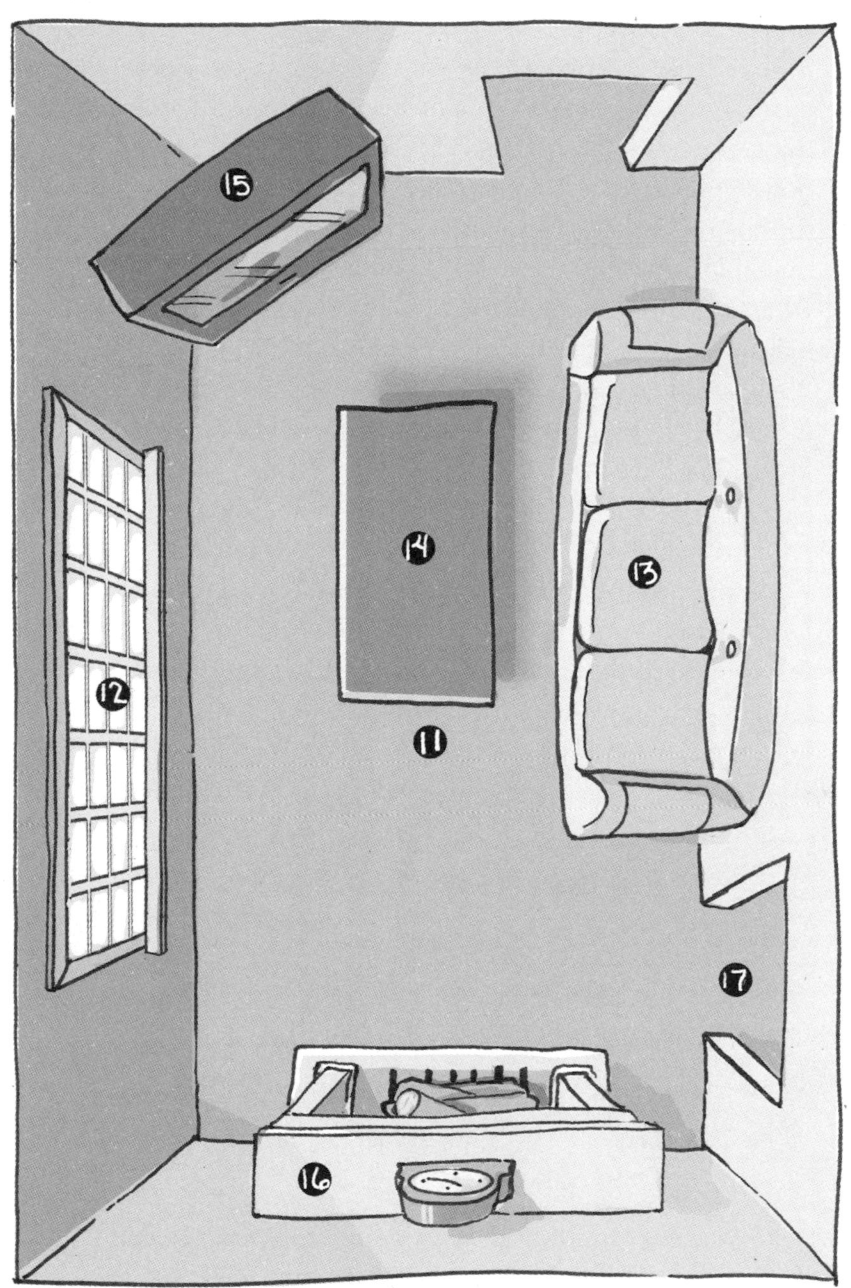

Living Room

happen to know a person named *Ezra* — the name of the next book — by all means place Ezra's face on the screen instead. The image in the fireplace brings a little disappointment at first. You think you spy the legs of Santa Claus himself, but on closer inspection you note, "Those are *my knees!*" Yes, the sixteenth book of the Bible is *Nehemiah*. The last location in the living room is at the threshold to the dining room. I'm going to call to mind the image we used in this location the first time through the house. Do you remember the giant sloth that represented the capital sin of sloth? Well, he just *bit* your *toe*. The seventeenth book of the Old Testament is *Tobit*. Recap a bit to recall that the seven locations of the living room have helped us lock in *1* and *2 Kings*, *1* and *2 Chronicles*, *Ezra*, *Nehemiah*, and *Tobit*. Then to the dining room and seven more books.

As we cross the threshold into the dining room we're met by a Jewish person offering us a dish of delicious food. *Jew-dish* will help us remember the book of *Judith*. Next, at the seat at the head of the table sits an enormous multicolored *Easter egg*, because Easter can help us remember *Esther*. (Again, if you know an Esther, you can substitute her image.) You notice next that in the center of the

THE BOOKS OF THE OLD TESTAMENT

Location	**Image**	**Book**
11. Center of living room	*Giant white chess king*	1 Kings
12. Picture window	*Giant black chess king*	2 Kings
13. Sofa	*Icicles*	1 Chronicles
14. Coffee table	*More icicles*	2 Chronicles
15. Big-screen TV	*Zebra*	Ezra
16. Fireplace	"*My knees*"	Nehemiah
17. Living-room doorway	*Sloth biting toe*	Tobit

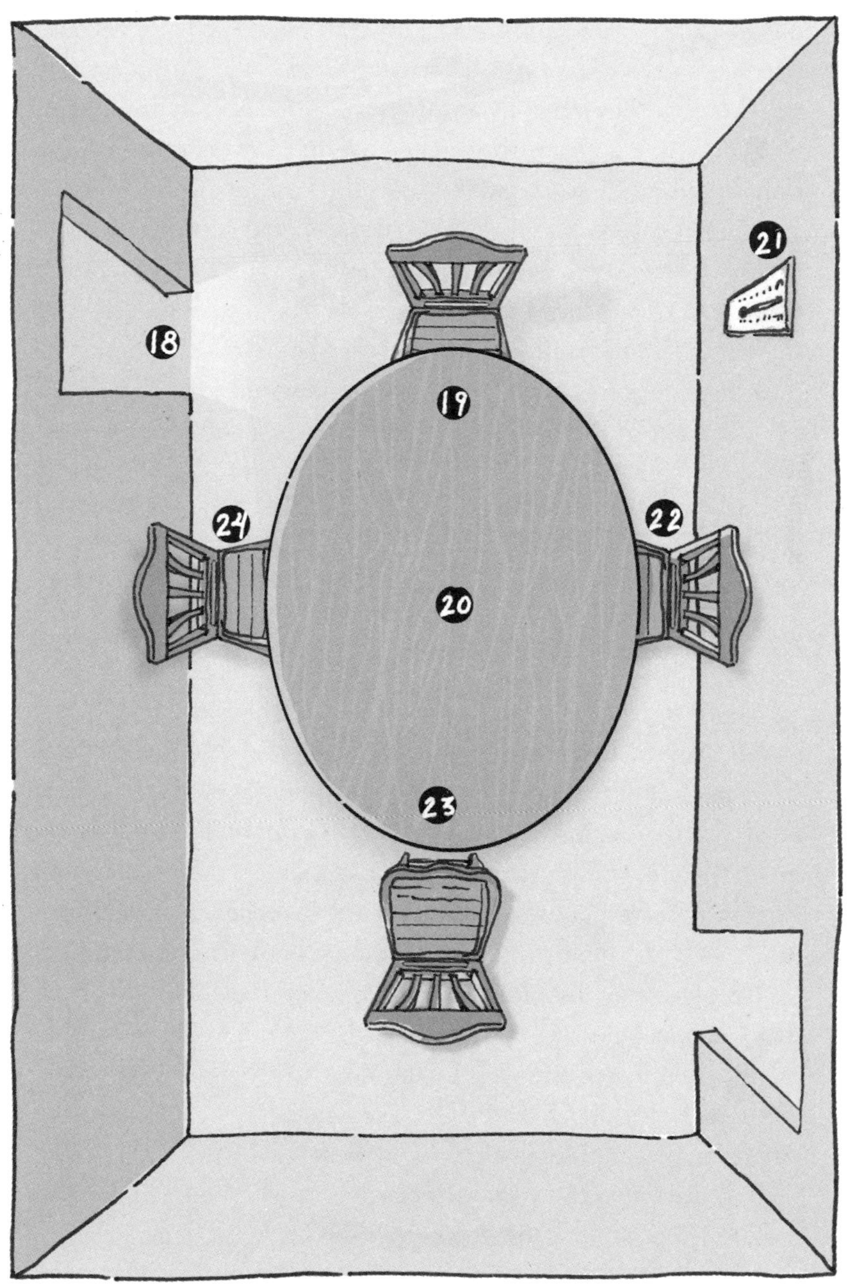

Dining Room

table, a huge fly swatter is smacking at a bunch of bees, because *smacking bees* will remind us of *Maccabees*. Not caring for the smacking, the bees then fly away to rest on the wall thermometer. Now, any time we have the same image in two consecutive locations, it tells us there are two books of the same name, in this case, *1* and *2 Maccabees*. Moving back to the second chair of the dining-room table, we see a man wearing a large "*Job wanted*" sign. What we want is to remember the book of *Job*. There is an odd sight at the tail end of the dining-room table, because several giant palm trees are perched on the chair. *Palms* will remind us of *Psalms*. At the last chair of the table is an even stranger sight. Does anyone recall the child's toy called "Furby" that was very popular in the late 1990s? Well, there's an assortment of deluxe, professional models of the furry little creatures sitting in that last chair — yes, "*Pro Furbies*." As far-fetched as it may seem, *Pro Furbies* will help us recall the book of *Proverbs* until we no longer need a mnemonic image.

Now, can you picture this scene again? We have the Jewish person with the dish, the Easter egg, smacking bees in two locations, the man looking for a job, the palm trees, and the Pro Furbies. The eighteenth through the twenty-fourth books of the Old Testament, then, are *Judith*, *Esther*, *1* and *2 Maccabees*, *Job*, *Psalms*, and *Proverbs*. We have more than half the books memorized now! This brings us to the family room and the nine books that it contains.

All right, at location 25 we begin to open the door to the family room, but we notice it shuts itself the second we let go. Someone has connected the edge of the door to the wall with *elastic*. The twenty-fifth book of the Old Testament, then, is *Ecclesiastes*. After you've carefully made your way into the room, you notice the tall dresser in the corner (location 26), and perched precariously on top is old King Solomon himself, boomingly *singing a song*. The book is the *Song of Solomon* (also known as the *Song of Songs*. On next to the smaller television set (27). An enormous

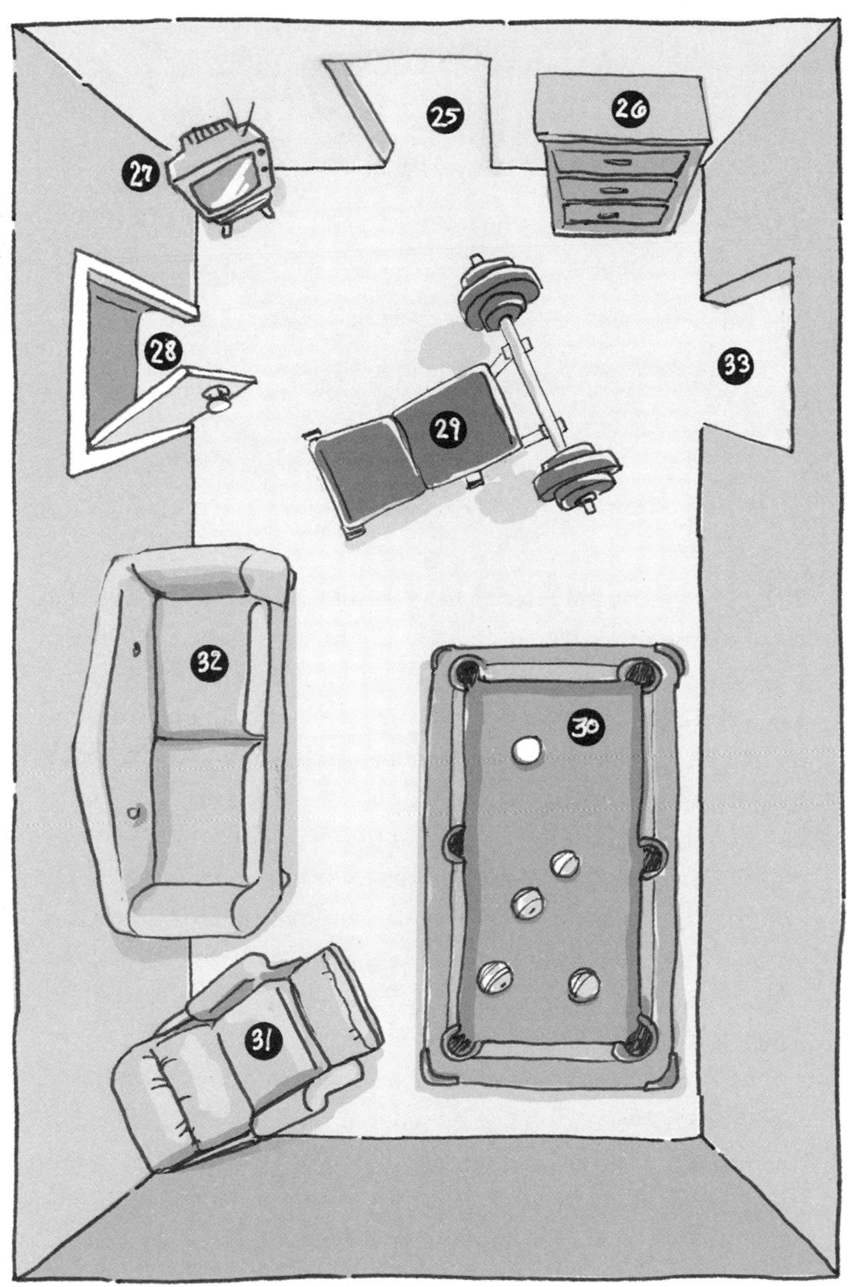

Family Room

THE BOOKS OF THE OLD TESTAMENT

Location	Image	Book
18. Dining-room doorway	*Jew offering dish*	Judith
19. Head of table	*Giant Easter egg*	Esther
20. Center of table	*Smacking bees*	1 Maccabees
21. Thermometer	*Smacking more bees*	2 Maccabees
22. Seat on right	*Man with "job wanted" sign*	Job
23. Foot of table	*Palm tree*	Psalms
24. Seat on left	*Pro Furbies*	Proverbs

image of a freshly pulled *wisdom tooth* fills the screen. You find that it's a commercial advertising a new dentist in town. The wisdom tooth is our concrete image for the book of *Wisdom*. Moving along, when you open the closet door (28), a man with a foreign accent, assuming you're looking for a rack of clothing, tells you "*Zee rack* is right here," because the book of *Sirach* is right here in our mnemonic system. You turn around and notice that another man is pinned under a large barbell on the weightlifting bench (29)! Except this time the man is not French, but English. He's quite calm about it too, and he calls out to you with his strong British accent, "*I say*, old man, would you give me a hand?" The book at the bench is the book of the prophet *Isaiah*.

Next we move to the pool table, location 30 in our house. I hope you know a person named Jeremiah whom you can place on the pool table. If not, you might have to use the first association that comes into my head. When I was young, a very popular song contained the strikingly unusual line, "Jeremiah was a bullfrog." (Another score for the idea that we tend to remember "unwonted" or unusual images.) Meaning no disrespect to the ancient prophet,

in my mnemonic system, there's a *bullfrog* on the pool table, and it has *never* failed to remind me of the book of *Jeremiah*.

On now to the recliner, wherein sits a *tearful lamb*. We have reached the book of *Lamentations*. Next we spy another animal on the couch. It looks like the bear we met the last time we saw this couch. (Perhaps this is why the lamb is tearful.) But on closer inspection we see that the animal on the couch is actually just a large *bear rug*, and the book it represents is *Baruch*. As we open the door to leave the family room, we see a third and final animal when the accented man from the closet points out to us "*zee eagle*." The thirty-third book of the Old Testament is *Ezekiel*.

To recap: elastic, Solomon singing, a wisdom tooth, "zee rack" of clothing, the trapped bench-presser's "I say, old man," the bullfrog, the lamb, the bear rug, and "zee eagle," lock in for us the twenty-fifth through thirty-third books — namely, *Ecclesiastes*, *Song of Solomon*, *Wisdom*, *Sirach*, *Isaiah*, *Jeremiah*, *Lamentations*, *Baruch*, and *Ezekiel*. We have covered about three-fourths of the books of the Old Testament now. Shall we continue on to meet the prophets in the cathedral?

Location 34 in our house, and the first in the cathedral, is the site of the baptismal font. Inside this font we see a man surrounded by *lions*. Are you familiar with the story of Daniel and the lion's

THE BOOKS OF THE OLD TESTAMENT

Location	Image	Book
25. Door to family room	*Elastic*	Ecclesiastes
26. Dresser	*Solomon singing*	Song of Solomon
27. Television	*Wisdom tooth*	Wisdom
28. Closet	*Man saying, "Zee rack is here"*	Sirach
29. Weightlifting bench	*British man saying, "I say, old man"*	Isaiah
30. Pool table	*Bullfrog*	Jeremiah
31. Recliner	*Crying lamb*	Lamentations
32. Couch	*Bear rug*	Baruch
33. Door to outside	*Man saying, "Zee eagle"*	Ezekiel

den? I hope so, since this is our image for the book of *Daniel*, wherein that story is told. Moving on to the center spot in front of the first row of pews, you notice a gigantic *fire hose*. Perhaps someone is preparing to shoo away those lions. Let this remind you that the thirty-fifth book of the Bible is *Hosea*.

On now to the altar. Let's imagine that it's Christmas Day and a banner in front of the altar proclaims, "*Noel!*" Picture a large *J* next to it if you like, to lock in the fact that the book is not Noel, but *Joel*. Moving to the side of the church, you conclude that the confessional booth has not been used as much as it should be, because it is completely covered with *a moss*. This book is *Amos*. Our next location is right in front of the right row of pews. A girl from the grade-school band is standing there playing an

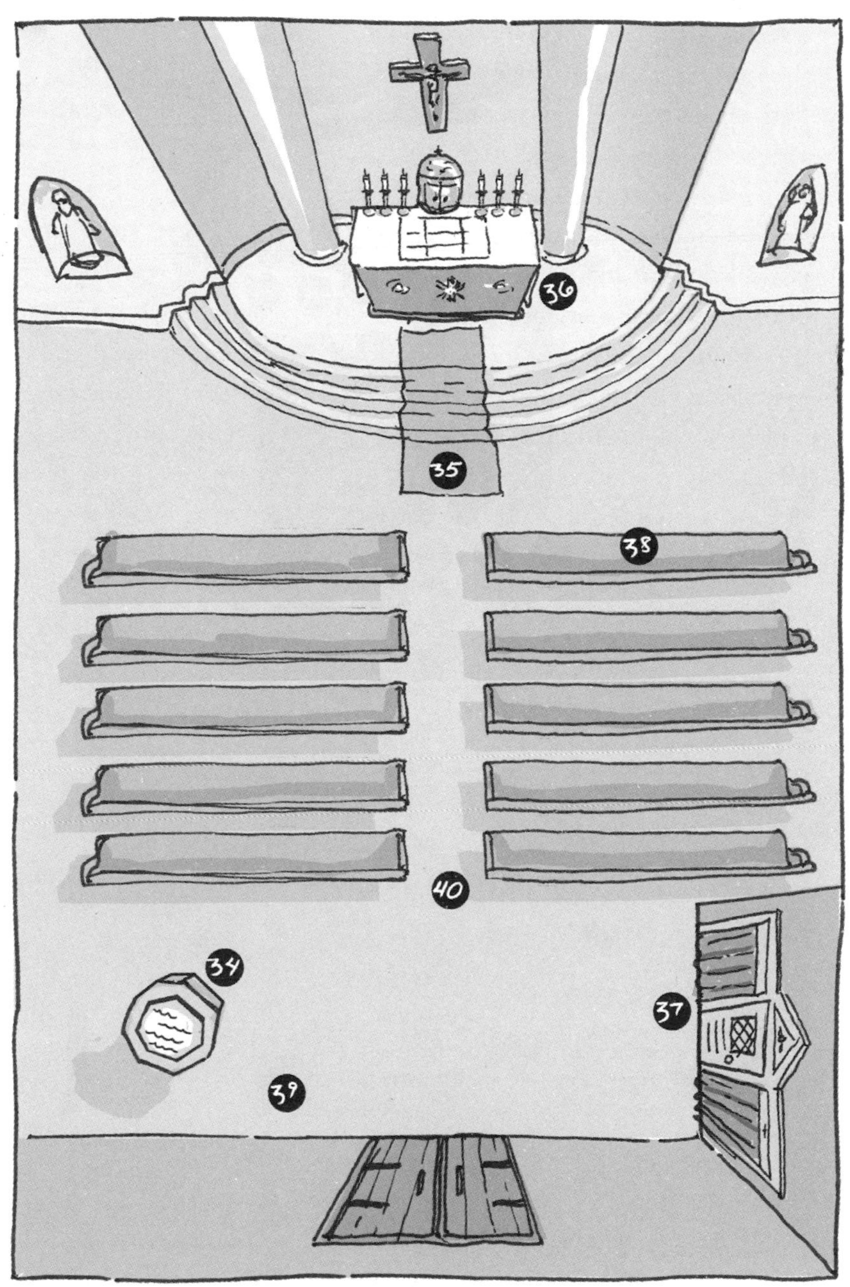

Cathedral

oboe. Unfortunately, a prankish schoolmate has placed some *dye* in the instrument and her first note blows out a stream on everybody in the front row. The unwonted image of *oboe* and *dye* should provide us the wanted association with the book of *Obadiah*.

There's a very striking sight at the back of the church. A man has just emerged from the *belly of a very large fish*. Who could that possibly be but *Jonah*? Finally, at the opposite end of the cathedral, at the beginning of the center aisle, is a figure in white. Yes, it's a beautiful bride, but most important, she's bending down and inspecting the floor. She determines that it's made of Formica, which she has been considering using for her kitchen counter. *Formica* is our mnemonic for *Micah*.

We've covered forty of the forty-six books now. We'll need only six of the twenty locations of the study to lock in the rest of

THE BOOKS OF THE OLD TESTAMENT

Location	Image	Book
34. Baptismal font	*Man surrounded by lions*	Daniel
35. Center front	*Huge fire hose aimed at lions*	Hosea
36. Altar	*Noel sign with J instead of* N	Joel
37. Confessional	*Covered in moss*	Amos
38. Front pew right	*Girl with oboe spitting out dye*	Obadiah
39. Back of church	*Man emerging from a great fish*	Jonah
40. Start of center aisle	*Bride examines Formica flooring*	Micah

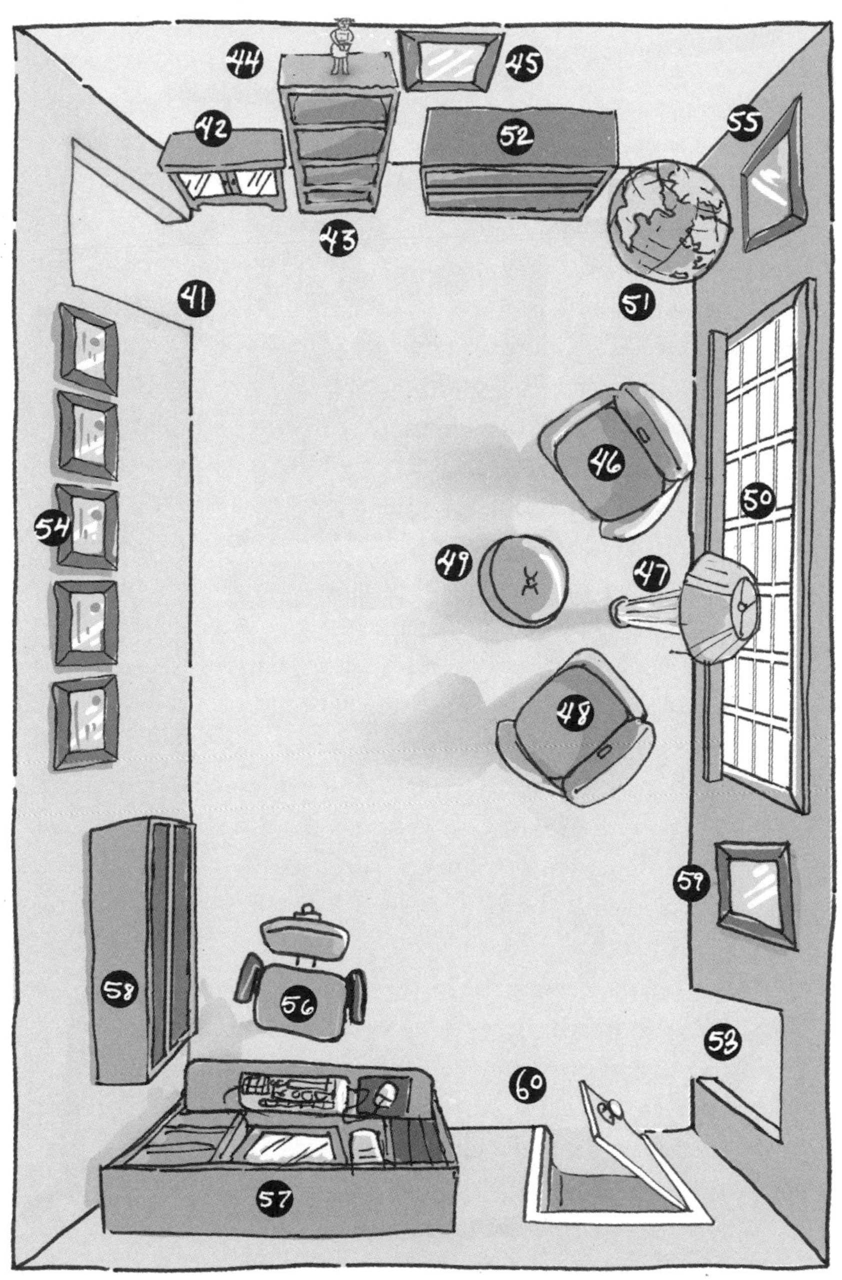

Study

the books. Let's recap the books of the cathedral first. The man surrounded by lions, the fire hose, the Noel with a *J* on the altar, the moss-covered confessional, the oboe emitting dye, Jonah emerging from the fish, and the bride inspecting the Formica flooring have helped us to learn books thirty-four through forty — namely, *Daniel, Hosea, Joel, Amos, Obadiah, Jonah,* and *Micah.*

As we open the door to the study, we feel a sense of relief that there are only six books to go. So happy that we begin to hum aloud, and the librarian who greets us at the door has to scold us mildly: "*No humming!*" The forty-first book, you see, is *Nahum.* Next, you notice that the librarian is wearing an apron and a chef's hat. She points to a large book in the small bookcase and says, "*Have a cookbook,*" because the forty-second book is *Habakkuk.* Moving over to the taller bookshelf, you notice a book with a very strange cover. Apparently meant to help children learn the letters of the alphabet, it pictures a lifelike *Z fanning an I.* The forty-third book is *Zephaniah.* Sitting atop that tall bookcase is a striking sculpture depicting the three fabled *hags* who shared one *eye.* The forty-fourth book is *Haggai.* Next, we move to the picture on the wall. Now, we've seen pictures of foods before, maybe apples or pears. The ancient Greeks told of paintings so lifelike that birds would fly down to try to eat the fruit. Our painting here, though, depicts a sack of rye flour, since a *sack of rye* will allow us to remember the book of *Zechariah.*

We've finally reached the forty-sixth and last book of the Old Testament. Spying the first swivel rocker, you're sure that a young child has just gotten up from it. Not only is it still rocking a bit, but you notice that a half-eaten bag of *marshmallows* and a rather sticky *kite* are sitting in the chair. *Mallow* and *kite*, you see, will remind us of *Malachi.*

Whew! We've covered them all now. Let's review the study. The librarian warning us "no humming," and suggesting "have a cookbook," the Z fanning the *I*, the hags with one eye, the sack of

THE BOOKS OF THE OLD TESTAMENT

Location	Image	Book
41. Study door	*"No humming!"*	Nahum
42. Short bookcase	*"Have a cookbook"*	Habakkuk
43. Tall bookcase	*Book with Z fanning I*	Zephaniah
44. Statue	*Three hags sharing one eye*	Haggai
45. Picture	*Sack of rye*	Zechariah
46. First chair	*Marshmallows and sticky kite*	Malachi

rye, and the mallow and the kite, silly as they are, have enabled us to memorize the forty-first through forty-sixth books of *Nahum, Habakkuk, Zephaniah, Haggai, Zechariah,* and *Malachi.*

Now we've covered them all. Take your time to do the practice and repetition necessary to lock them all in. I strongly suggest mastering one room at a time before moving on. And yes, when you really get these down, you'll find that you also know them backward. When you've mastered all the locations and their numbers, if someone calls out the book of say, *Esther*, you'll know that *Esther* is, in fact, the nineteenth book of the Bible and that it's preceded by *Judith* and followed by *1 Maccabees*. Although you'll probably rarely be asked to call out these books by their number, I think you'll find that knowing them in order can speed your ability to look up desired texts. How to remember *the exact location of those text passages, as well as their exact words*, will be addressed in chapters ahead. For now, I'll simply point out the main purpose of memorizing the names of these books is to inspire us to learn what is in them!

MEMORY MASTER TIPS AND FACTS

QUESTION 21

Can you elaborate a bit more on working memory?

The concept of working memory emphasizes that short-term memory can be a very active process, especially when we're trying to do more than one thing at a time. Take, for example, the "digit span" test I mentioned earlier. This involves repeating strings of digits aloud. I say, 9843625, for example, and you say 9843625. A simple test that begins to tap into working memory capacity is "digit span backward." I say another number such as 7396528, and your task is to repeat the digits in reverse order, 8256937. Do you see that this more difficult task demands more concentration and mental juggling?

Some major historical figures have displayed incredible working memory capacities by their ability to dictate aloud to several secretaries, on several different topics. While one wrote, the speaker dictated to another, and so on. After dictating to three or four of them, he would go back around to each man and continue where he had left off with that man. Two men who reportedly dictated this way were Julius Caesar and St. Thomas Aquinas.

Chapter 22

The Twenty-Seven Books of the New Testament

"The Word of God, which is the power of God for salvation to everyone who has faith, is set forth and displays it power in a most wonderful way in the writings of the New Testament, which hand on the ultimate truth in God's Revelation."

Catechism of the Catholic Church, 124

The Old Testament stores profound memories of relevance, not only for Jews and Christians, but for all mankind. I hope the names of those books are now stored in your memory and you're ready to explore them in more depth. But, of course, there's more to the Sacred Scriptures. The Old Testament prepared for and prophesied the coming of Jesus Christ, and the New Testament tells his story. So, in our pursuit of "ultimate truth," let's return to our mnemonic house one more time. The forty-six books of the Old Testament required all six rooms; the twenty-seven books of the New Testament will require fewer locations and much less square footage — just four rooms in all.

I assume that the first four books of the New Testament will require no mnemonic for most readers. "Matthew, Mark, Luke, and John" rolls easily off the tongue. Perhaps a few readers have reflexively added, "Bless this bed that I lie on," forever remembering

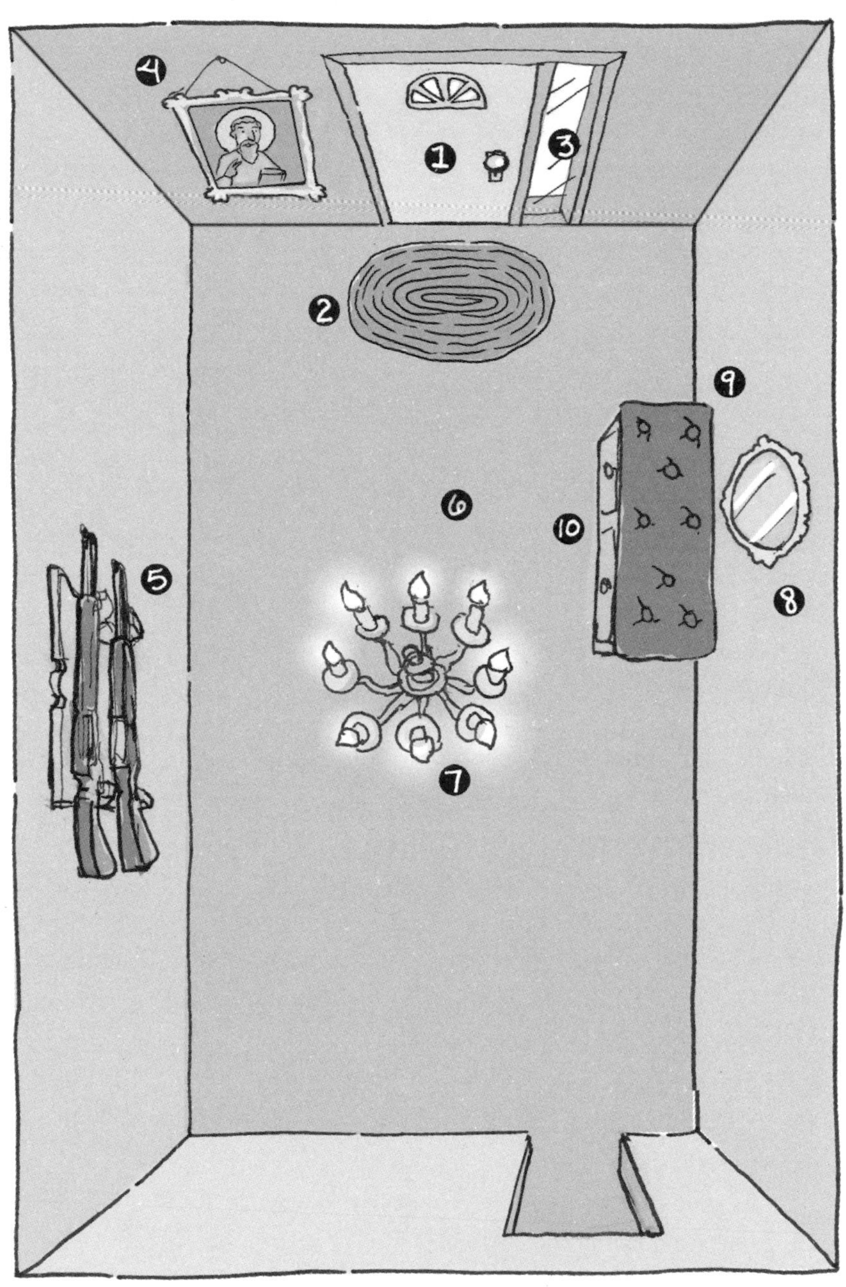

Foyer

that childhood prayer. In case you do not have this familiarity, I'll provide some images. This will also keep us in sequence as we remember these books by number and in their exact order.

Let's imagine that when you come to the front door of the house (location 1), you notice a welcome mat, not on the ground in front of the door, but hanging straight down from it. *Mat* reminds us of *Matthew*. Next, on the doormat (2), you notice a large unusual *mark* to remind us of *Mark*. (If you know a Mark, you could, of course, picture his face on the mat.) Looking out the pane-glass window next to the door (3), who do we see but Luke Skywalker of "Star Wars" fame! *Luke Skywalker,* of course, represents for us not a space warrior, but the book of the "beloved physician" and evangelist, *Luke*. Next, we're on to the portrait on the wall of the foyer (4). Surely you know a person named *John*. Please put his portrait here to remind you of the Gospel of *John*.

Next, you notice that the gun rack on the wall (5) holds not guns, but a very large *ax*, representing the *Acts of the Apostles*.

In the center of the foyer (6) you notice a large stack of *letters* with a Minnesota return address — *St. Paul,* to be exact. The top letter is addressed to the *Romans*, and there's a man in a toga reading it. The sixth book of the New Testament, then, is St. Paul's letter to the Romans (or *Romans* for short). Looking up at the chandelier (7), you notice that instead of candles or lightbulbs, there are glowing miniature Grecian columns. You can tell by the ornate pattern at their tops that these are, in fact, *Corinthian columns*. The seventh book is St. Paul's first letter to the Corinthians, or simply *1 Corinthians*. Next, when you look at the mirror (8), you see not your own reflection, but those same *Corinthian columns again*. The eighth book, then, is St. Paul's second letter to the Corinthians, or *2 Corinthians*.

Moving next to the bench under the mirror (9), you notice a huge pair of muddy *galoshes* that will serve to remind you of the letter to the *Galatians*. Last in the foyer is the drawer of the bench

THE BOOKS OF THE NEW TESTAMENT

Location	Image	Book
1. Front door	*Mat hanging on door*	Matthew
2. Doormat	*Face of a Mark you know on it*	Mark
3. Glass panel	*Luke Skywalker of* Star Wars	Luke
4. Portrait	*A John you know*	John
5. Gun rack	*Axes instead of guns*	Acts of the Apostles
6. Center of foyer	*Roman and letter/ St. Paul return address*	Romans
7. Chandelier	*Ornate Corinthian columns for candles*	1 Corinthians
8. Mirror	*Reflection of Corinthian columns*	2 Corinthians
9. Bench	*Muddy galoshes*	Galatians
10. Drawer	*Little Parisians with Es on shirts*	Ephesians

(10). When you open this drawer, you're quite surprised to see a multitude of tiny Parisians — yes, small Frenchmen wearing berets. Part of the surprise comes from the fact that you didn't think St. Paul wrote to the people of Paris. Well, you're right, but these Parisians have very large *E*s on their shirts. They're trying to remind us not of themselves, but of the *Ephesians*. Get it? "*E Parisians*"? Oh well, sometimes the most strained mnemonic images work best because of the effort they involve.

To recap before settling in to the living room: the mat on the door reminds us of *Matthew*, the mark on the doormat is for *Mark*,

Luke Skywalker represents *Luke*, our friend John reminds us of *John*, an ax for *Acts*, a Roman for *Romans*, Corinthian columns for *1 Corinthians*, more columns for *2 Corinthians*, galoshes for *Galatians*, and Parisians for *Ephesians*. Now we have the first ten books of the New Testament. Let's see what's in store (I mean house) next.

In the center of the living room (11) is a man doing a *flip*. (For extra effect, if you know a person named Philip, picture him doing the flip.) The eleventh book, still another of the letters of Paul, is *Philippians*. Next you see a most disconcerting sight when you look out the picture window (12). Are you familiar with the enormous *Colossus of Rhodes*? This massive statue of Apollo in the bay of the Greek island of Rhodes was one of the wonders of the ancient world, a forerunner of our colossal Statue of Liberty. Just picture that *colossus* taking up half the backyard, towering over the oaks, with his head in the clouds. This striking image will help you remember that the twelfth book of the New Testament is the letter to the *Colossians*.

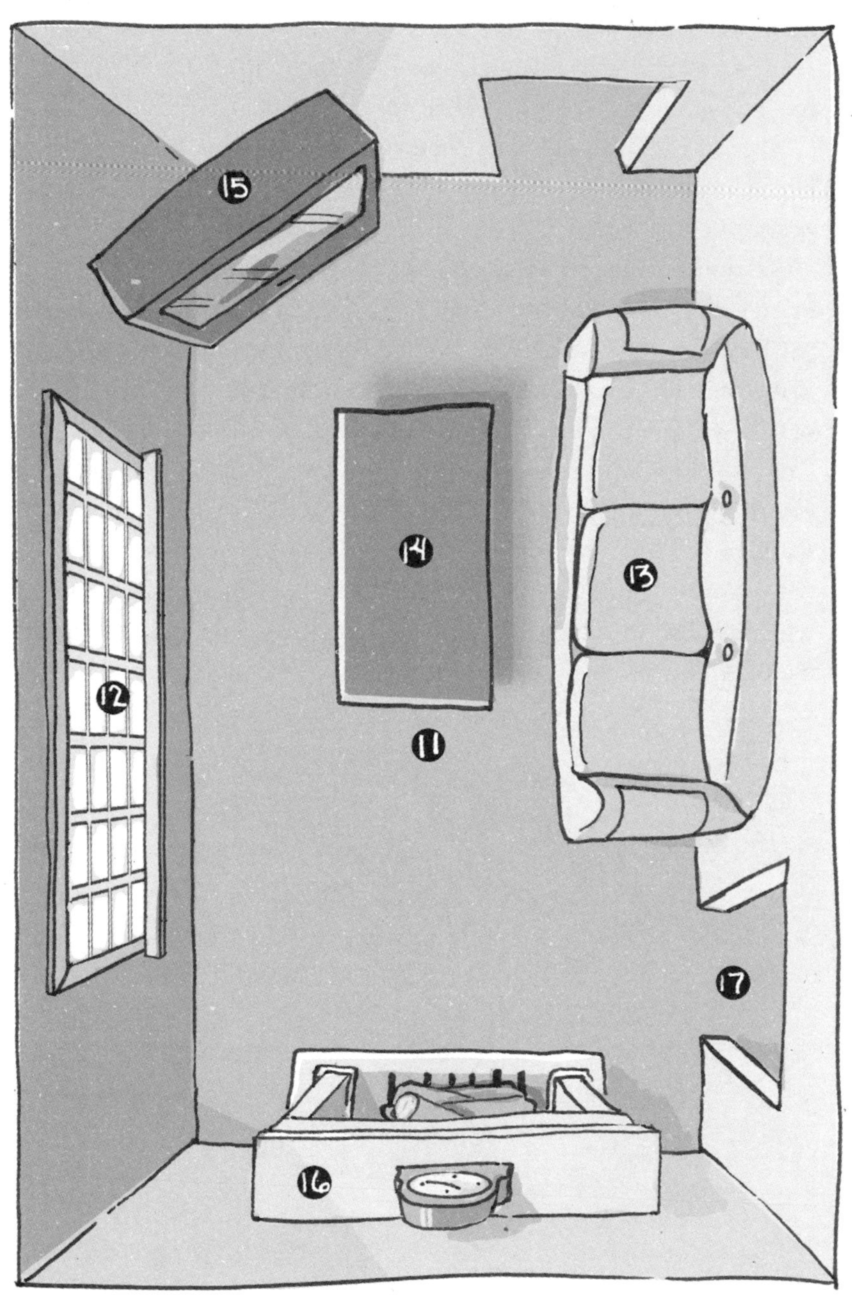

Living Room

On to the sofa (13) we see a calmer, gentler image. When I was little, my mother would sometimes take me with her when she went to the "beauty salon." Can you picture the women sitting in a salon under old-fashioned hair dryers? Picture them sitting on the sofa under those dryers, and odder still, picture a few more sitting on the coffee table (14). If you can imagine them in these two locations, the "salon-ians" will help you remember two more of St. Paul's letters: *1* and *2 Thessalonians*.

We next move right into yet another pair of St. Paul's letters. When I think of a Timothy, the first thought from my childhood is of the old television show *Timmy and Lassie*. Picture little Timmy on the big-screen TV (15), hopping right out of the screen to pet Lassie, who's sitting in front of the fireplace (16). *Timmy*, in two consecutive locations reminds me of *1* and *2 Timothy*, and I hope it

THE BOOKS OF THE NEW TESTAMENT

Location	Image	Book
11. Center of living room	*Phil doing a flip*	Philippians
12. Picture window	*Colossus of Rhodes in backyard*	Colossians
13. Sofa	*Ladies under dryer in hair salon*	1 Thessalonians
14. Coffee table	*More "salon-ians" sitting there*	2 Thessalonians
15. Big-screen TV	*Lassie's friend Timmy*	1 Timothy
16. Fireplace	*Timmy walks to fire-place to pet Lassie*	2 Timothy
17. Living-room doorway	*Giant Greek Titan*	Titus

will remind you too. The last book in the living room sits at the doorway to the dining room (17), and believe it or not, here we meet another ancient giant — a Titan to be exact. In ancient Greek mythology, the Titans were the older race of gods who preceded the Olympians. Can you picture a Titan, such as Atlas, who held up the world, holding up the doorway to the dining room? Just be sure that you remember not Atlas, but *Titan*, because the next book of the New Testament is the letter to *Titus*.

So what did the living room hold? The eleventh through seventeenth books of the New Testament: Phillip doing a flip for *Philippians*, the mighty Colossus of Rhodes for the letter to the *Colossians*, "the salon-ians" with their hair dryers for *1* and *2 Thessalonians*, Lassie's friend Timmy in two locations for *1* and *2 Timothy*, and a massive Titan for *Titus*. All these books, you'll recall, were letters written by St. Paul. (Sorry for sounding like Dr. Seuss, but a few too many mnemonics and your brain gets loose.)

As we enter the doorway of the dining room (18) we're met with one last image of Greek mythology to help us recall a book of the New Testament. (Two asides to defend their use: St. Paul wrote these letters in Greek; and many Christians writers, including such well-loved moderns as G. K. Chesterton and C. S. Lewis, have noted that in some ways the myths of Greeks and Romans foreshadowed or hinted at truths to be revealed in Christianity.)

So what is the next image? Do you recall the name for the mythological creature that was half-man and half-horse? Yes, the centaur. But that isn't exactly our image. Our imaginary human-equine mixture must be half man, but half *female* horse, or "filly," because if we can imagine a *"filly man,"* we can remember St. Paul's letter to his friend *Philemon*.

On to the head of the table. Here a man with a Jewish skullcap is *brewing coffee*. Delighting in the aroma, you can't help but exclaim, *"He brews well!"* This represents, of course, none other than the letter to the *Hebrews*, the last of the epistles of St. Paul.

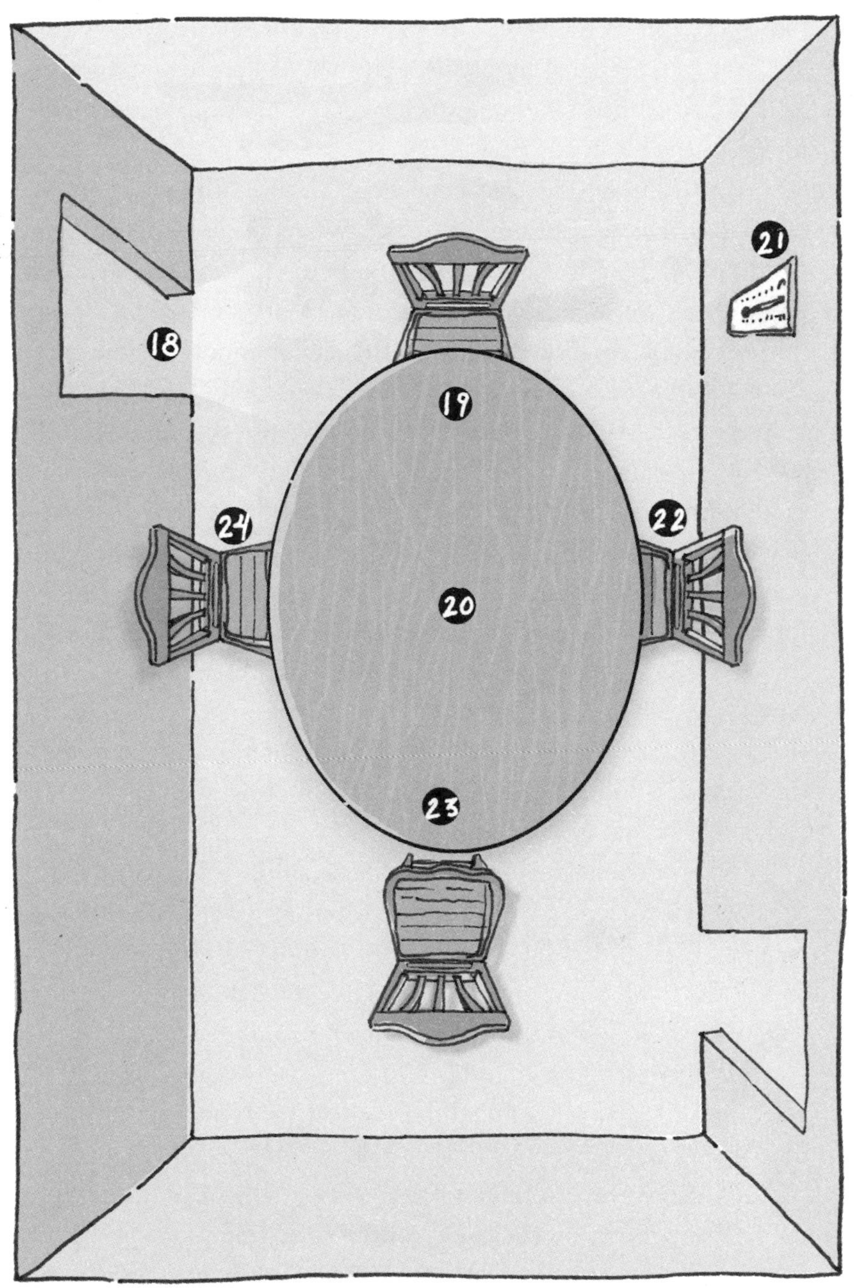

Dining Room

On the center of the table sits your friend or relative James (or even you, if your name should happen to be James). Don't know a James? Just substitute a large stack of games. *James* or *games* will represent the letter of *James*.

Did you know that the name Peter derives from the Greek word *petra*, meaning "stone" or "rock"? We retain in it the English word *petrify*. Jesus gave the name of Peter to Simon when he named him as the "rock" of his church (Matt. 16:18). Can you imagine a huge rock emerging from the wall thermometer and extending to the next chair of the dining-room table? If so, this will help you recall that the twenty-first and twenty-second books of the New Testament are St. Peter's letters, *1* and *2 Peter*.

Finishing the dining room is a set of triplets, and all of them are named John. Please use the same John you used as the image in the portrait for the book of John, because they represent the same John, but there must be three Johns now, in the chair at the foot of the table (23); at the chair opposite Peter, the rock (24); and — jumping ahead one location into the next room — holding open the door to the family room (25). These three Johns represent three letters of John the Evangelist, and they bring us almost to the end of the Bible.

We'll take a quick peek, then, into the family room to see that the dresser (26) is made not of wood, but of jewels. It is in fact completely jeweled, and *jeweled* will stand for *Jude*. Finally, as we look at the small television set (27), we observe the most amazing scene we could ever imagine: *Jesus himself coming in a cloud of glory — revealing himself to the world*. This scene is, of course, from the book of *Revelation* (also called the Apocalypse), the last book in the Bible.

Let's review the last ten books now. The "filly man" stands for the letter to *Philemon*. The man brewing coffee reminded us of the letter to the *Hebrews*, the James (or games) in the center of the table remind us of the letter of *James*, the rock extended from the

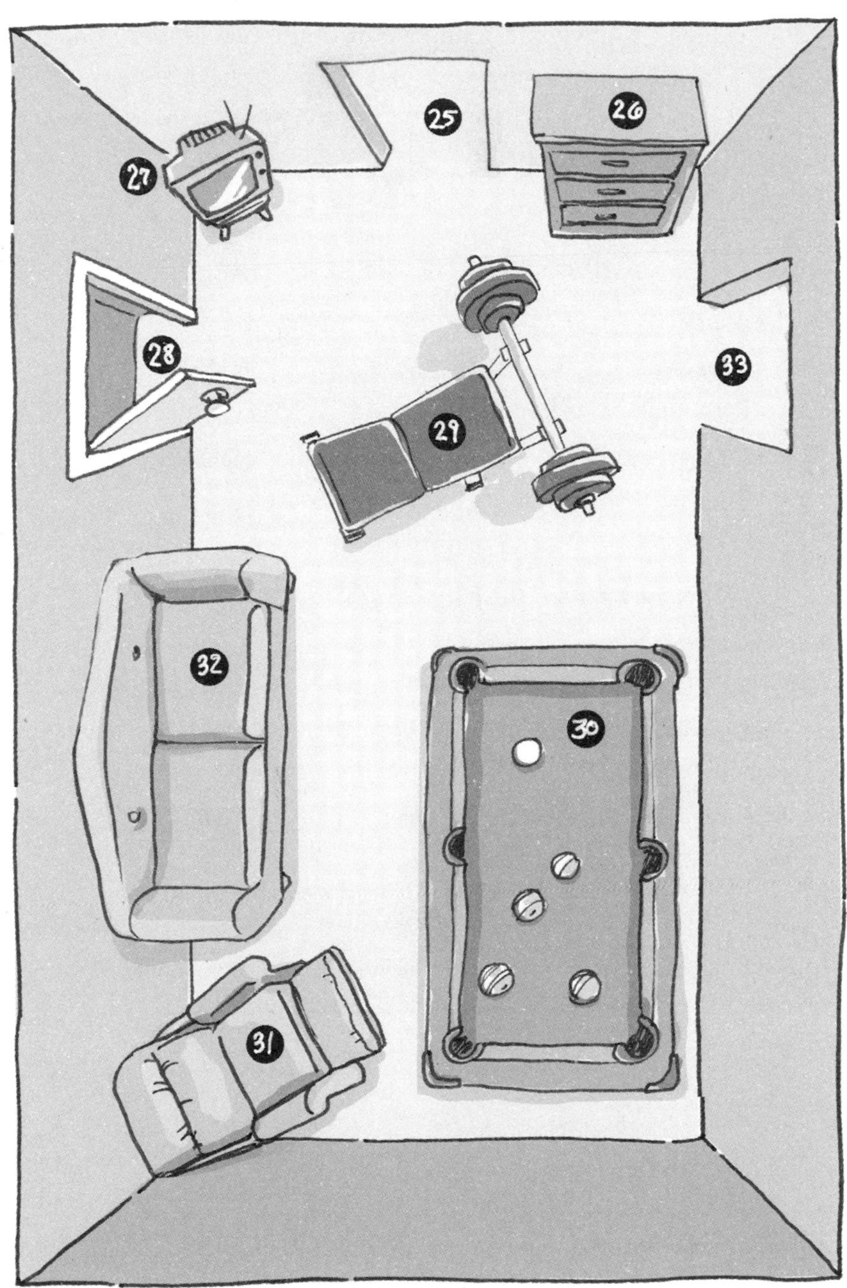

Family Room

thermometer to the chair reminded us of the two letters *1* and *2 Peter*, the three Johns remind us of *1*, *2*, and *3 John*, the jeweled dresser reminds us of *Jude*, and finally, Jesus coming on the cloud depicted on television reminds us of the book of *Revelation*.

THE BOOKS OF THE NEW TESTAMENT

Location	Image	Book
18. Dining-room entrance	*"Filly-man"*	Philemon
19. Head of table	*"He brews coffee well"*	Hebrews
20. Center of table	*Your friend James or games*	James
21. Thermometer	*It's turned to solid rock*	1 Peter
22. Dining-room chair	*The rock extends to the chair*	2 Peter
23. Chair at end of table	*Your friend John again*	1 John
24. Last of four chairs	*Another John*	2 John
25. Family-room door	*A third John*	3 John
26. Tall dresser	*Covered with jewels*	Jude
27. Small TV	*Jesus coming on cloud of glory*	Revelation

Thus concludes the loci presentation for the books of the Bible. Considering both Testaments, that's seventy-three books in all — no small feat of memorization. It will probably take some additional practice to learn them, and it will definitely take some practice to retain them over time. Although I encourage you to rehearse the mnemonic images in the days and weeks ahead, the very best way to lock them in for good is to read these books of the Bible again and again throughout your lifetime.

MEMORY MASTER TIPS AND FACTS

QUESTION 22

Is it true that St. Thomas Aquinas condemned one ancient book on memory?

In the days before the printing press, the powers of memory were extremely important among the learned. Books were relatively scarce, so scholars like St. Thomas often committed vast sections of rare books to memory, when they had the chance. The memory powers of some mnemonic experts seemed downright magical to some people, and there were some memory experts who tried to capitalize on this misconception. They tied their techniques to occult practices such as astrology and alchemy. This is the kind of misrepresentation and misuse of mnemonics that St. Thomas decried, and this is why he condemned the *Ars Notoria* of Apollonius.

Chapter 23

Twenty-One Centuries of Church History

*"You are Peter, and on this rock I will build my Church.
And the powers of death shall not prevail against it."*
Matthew 16:18

Have you ever heard anyone say that the problem with Catholics is that they don't know the Bible, and the problem with Protestants is that they don't know Christian history? Well, the spiritual legacy of the Catholic Church has spanned some two thousand years now, and I wonder how much even lifelong Catholics know about their legacy (we still don't know enough about the Bible). Church history comprises such a tremendous amount of information that no one person could know it all. (The libraries of the Vatican alone contain two millennia's worth of original documents that fill miles of bookshelves.) Is there a way, though, that we could commit to memory some kind of general outline of important events, doctrines, and personalities in Church history? A simple framework that could be pieced together in one sitting, but could continue to build and grow throughout our lifetime? I have one for you that might do the trick.

One of the tremendous blessings of the Catholic Church is the Communion of Saints. So many thousands of people throughout the ages have sought to imitate Christ, gracing their eras with their unique personalities and gifts. A complete catalogue of these saints, of course, would be too vast and unwieldy for most of us to store in memory. But a realistic option would be to memorize a manageable number of especially prominent Church Fathers and saints throughout the centuries, as framework for a broader mental summary of Church history.

Every so often there will appear on earth, perhaps not for a hundred years or more, and then sometimes in a cluster of three or four within a single lifespan, a saint so intellectually blessed, so skilled at transmitting and deepening our understanding of theological and moral doctrines that he or she is officially proclaimed a "Doctor of the Church" (*doctor* deriving from the Latin word for *teacher*). There have only been thirty or so of these Doctors to date. I propose including eleven of these great teachers as part of our mnemonic framework of Church history. The list is somewhat arbitrary, focusing more on the Doctors I'm most familiar with, and starting with the earliest Doctor and ending with the last, in order to cover the broadest possible sweep of Church history, but all of these great saints and Doctors are worthy of our attention. For centuries without a Doctor I'll substitute some other great saint or pope, in order to fill out our twenty-one locations for twenty-one centuries of Catholic history. Please note that this could well prove to be the most useful mnemonic in this book — a very important set of loci that you can build on for years to come. I'll explain in due course.

For our mnemonic on Church history, I'm going to make use of the first twenty-one locations in our mnemonic house. Our technique will lock in not only the Doctors and other great saints, but also their greatest claims to fame, and the centuries in which they were born.

We'll slightly modify our usual tour through the house because we're going to remember a historical chronology, as well as persons

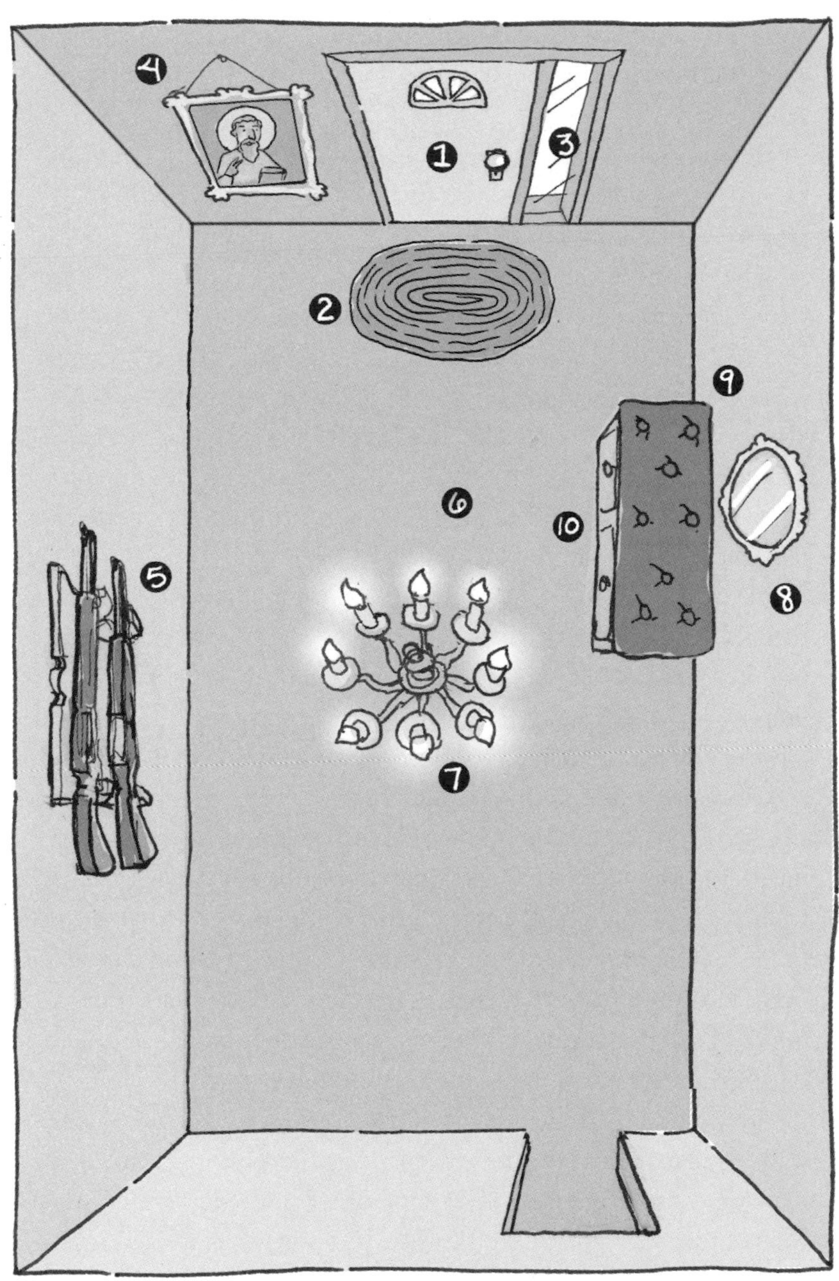

Foyer

and concepts. Each location will represent a century. The first location (front door) represents the first century (from 0 through 99 AD).

Let's imagine a huge *rock* here, since our first person to remember is *St. Peter the apostle*, the first pope, the rock upon which Christ's Church was built.

The second location represents the second century. So, here we will picture a great saint born between the years 100 and 199, and my choice is *Clement of Alexandria*, a learned Church Father who wrote the fascinating book *An Exhortation to the Greeks*. It demonstrates as profound a knowledge of the great classical Greco-Roman world as of the developing Christian canon. To remember Clement and the second century, let's picture a giant, juicy *clementine orange* sitting on the doormat.

Next we come to *St. Athanasius*, the earliest of the great Church Fathers to be declared a Doctor of the Church, born in 297. He was an extremely important figure in Church history for his triumph over the Arian heresy, which denied the full divinity of Christ. This powerful heresy almost overwhelmed the Church and the Roman Empire during Athanasius's lifetime. Since Athanasius was born in the third century, we'll connect his mnemonic image to the glass panel, the third location. Let's imagine that when we look out the glass into the front yard we see an *anesthetist* (a medical person who administers pain killers) pulling an *arrow* from the wound of an ancient Christian. *Anesthetist* is our reminder for Athanasius, and the arrow in the Christian represents the Arianism that was afflicting the Church.

On now to the fourth century and thus to the picture on the wall of the foyer. Picture the great *St. Augustine* himself, if you can remember seeing a representation of him. If not, picture *Augustus Caesar*, toga-clad and all, and picture him stepping out of a *confessional*, since St. Augustine is perhaps best known for his book *Confessions*.

Under the gun rack, we spy the *mane of a great lion*, since the fifth century boasts the birth of *Pope St. Leo the Great.* And great indeed was this lion of the Church. Picture the lion scaring away Attila the Hun, for one of this great pope's feats was indeed to turn Attila and his hordes from the gates of Rome.

On now to the center of the foyer, and in our sixth location we'll picture *Gregory the Great.* Do you know a Gregory? If so, elevate his image to greatness and sit him in the chandelier. Better yet, imagine him writing great works and corresponding with all the great churches of Christendom, or picture him chanting Gregorian chant. Pope St. Gregory the Great was known for his writings and for his close contact with churches throughout the world.

The seventh location is the chandelier, and here we see, shall I say, the "*darndest scene,*" for the great thinker of the Eastern Church, *St. John Damascene*, is sitting in the chandelier writing great works.

Location 8 is the mirror, and here we see our good friend *Al cooing* like a bird. The eighth century, you see, is represented by

TWENTY-ONE CENTURIES OF CHURCH HISTORY

Location	Image	Saint (Doctors in boldface)
1. Front door	*Huge rock*	St. Peter (d. 64)
2. Doormat	*Clementine orange*	Clement of Alexandria (150-217)
3. Glass panel	*Anesthetist*	**St. Athanasius** (296-373)
4. Portrait	*Picture of Augustine*	**St. Augustine** (354-430)
5. Gun rack	*Great lion*	**St. Leo the Great** (400-461)
6. Center of foyer	*A Greg you know*	**St. Gregory the Great** (540-604)
7. Chandelier	*"Darndest scene"*	**St. John Damascene** (645-749)
8. Mirror	*Al cooing*	St. Alcuin (735-804)
9. Bench	*Santa Claus*	St. Nicholas I (825-867)
10. Drawer	*Song "King Wenceslas"*	St. Wenceslas (907-929)

the Benedictine scholar and adviser to Charlemagne, *St. Alcuin.* He was a key figure in the rebirth of European learning, although, interestingly, it appears that he was *not* aware of the classical art of memory. His advice to maximize memory was merely to practice memorizing, writing, and studying (as well as "the avoidance of drunkenness!").

On now to the ninth century and the bench in the foyer. Who should be sitting there but *jolly old St. Nicholas* himself? Our figure for this century is Pope St. Nicholas I. This particular St. Nicholas (not "Santa Claus") did much to enhance and delineate the powers of the papacy. When you open the drawers in the bench at the tenth location, you're again reminded of Christmas, for the song "Good King Wenceslas" begins to play. This Slavic king, born in the tenth century, is a sainted martyr.

Next we move into the living room, and the eleventh location in its center is a saint most easily pictured. All you must do is imagine an *enormous dog*; of course, it must be a *St. Bernard*, for the eleventh century is when this famous Cistercian abbot and Doctor of the Church was born. The twelfth location is the picture window (note how this mnemonic location worked out quite fortuitously!). When you look through the window into the backyard, you see a sight not uncommon in backyards of the devout: a statue of *St. Francis of Assisi*, with birds hopping and chirping nearby, as if out of affection for this gentle nature-loving saint.

We skip now to the thirteenth location, and here resting comfortably on the sofa is our beloved guide himself, perhaps the greatest Doctor of all, *St. Thomas Aquinas*. You can imagine the other *sofa cushions weighted down* by the volumes of his *Summas*, if you like. Mine sometimes are. (The thirteenth century, by the way, was particularly rich in Doctors of the Church. Thomas's teacher Albert the Great and his friend St. Bonaventure could also join him on the sofa.)

On to location 14, the coffee table, and sitting there, carrying on a *dialogue* with God, is a very special guest. She's the first woman to grace this mnemonic with her presence: none other than *St. Catherine of Siena*. Do you recall an image of St. Catherine? If not, picture a Catherine you know. Have her proclaiming herself a *sinner*, and you'll remember she's from Siena. The *dialogue* will remind you of her great spiritual work by the same title.

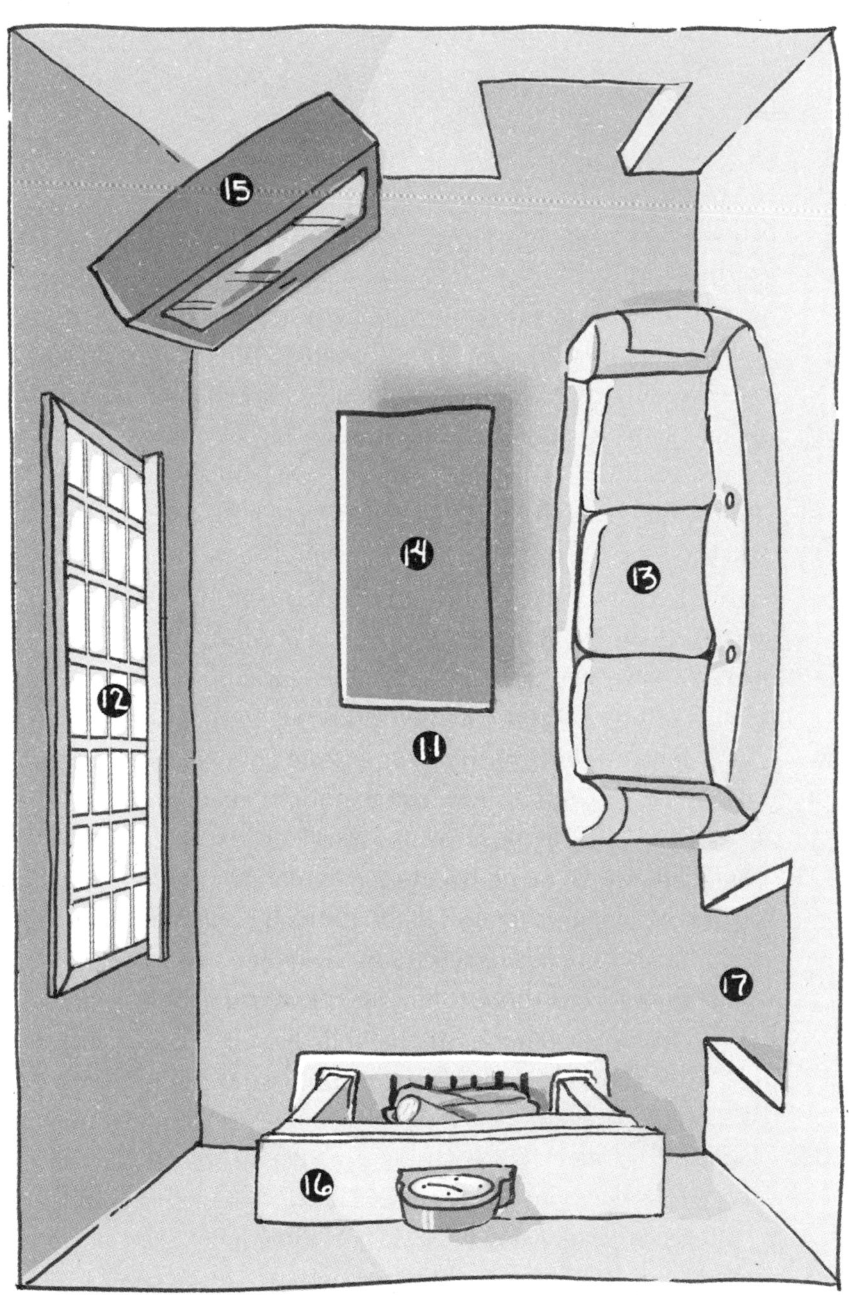

Living Room

The fifteenth location is the big-screen TV, and it looks as if we're just in time to watch an epic on the life of *St. Joan of Arc.* This brave young girl is the patron of soldiers and of France.

We skip now to the sixteenth century and thus location 16, the fireplace. You notice that it has grown very *dark* outside, and a very special man is picking up a *cross* to carry up a *mountain. St. John of the Cross*, you see, wrote two of the greatest works of mystical experience in the history of the Church — namely, the *Dark Night of the Soul* and *Ascent of Mount Carmel.*

The seventeenth location is the doorway to the dining room. Picture an *elephant* drinking from a large bottle of *liquor*. (In my hometown, there actually is a huge statue of just such a thing — and, yes, the elephant is pink). We're using this image, though, not to sell alcohol, but to remember *St. Alphonsus Liguori.* This bishop, missionary, and founder of a religious order suffered much, and, being a Doctor of the Church, he left us great theological writings.

TWENTY-ONE CENTURIES OF CHURCH HISTORY

Location	Image	Saint (Doctors in boldface)
11. Center of living room	*St. Bernard dog*	**St. Bernard of Clairvaux** (1090-1153)
12. Picture window	*St. Francis statue*	St. Francis of Assisi (1181-1226)
13. Sofa	*St. Thomas Aquinas*	**St. Thomas Aquinas** (1225-1274)
14. Coffee table	*A Cathy/"sinner"*	**St. Catherine of Siena** (1347-1380)
15. Big-screen TV	*Joan of Arc epic*	St. Joan of Arc (1412-1431)
16. Fireplace	*Man with cross*	**St. John of the Cross** (1542-1591)
17. Living-room doorway	*Elephant with liquor*	**St. Alphonsus Liguori** (1696-1787)

The eighteenth location is just inside the dining room and there's an evergreen tree growing right up through the carpet — a *juniper*, to be exact. The devoted missionary *Bl. Junipero Serra* spread the church through the West Coast of the United States. He's now the namesake of an organization promoting religious vocations.

The last of our great Doctors would probably insist on calling herself the least, although her small ways have had great impact on the faithful. Picture at the nineteenth location, the head chair of the dining-room table, the most beautiful *bouquet of small flowers* you've ever seen. This will remind you of *St. Thérèse of Lisieux*,

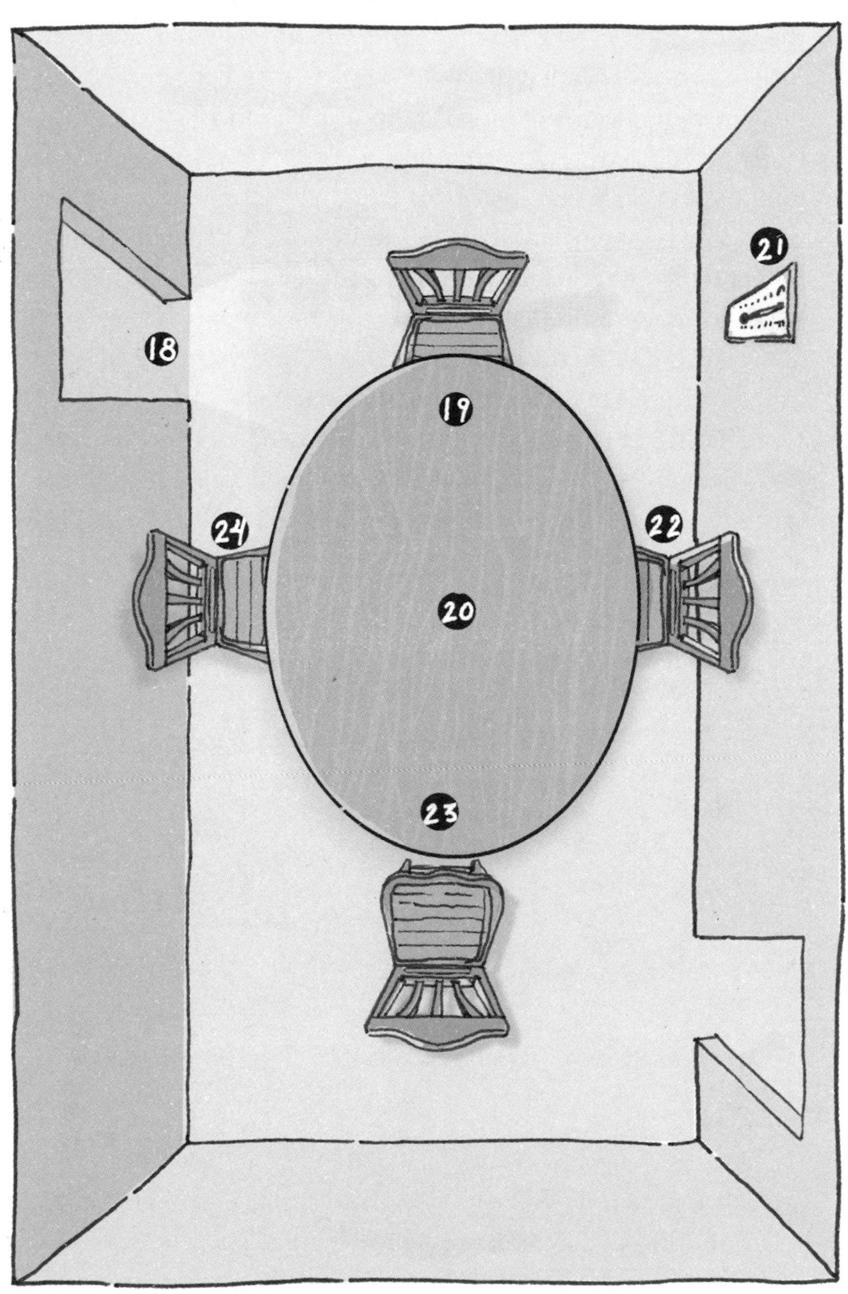

Dining Room

the "Little Flower." We'll discuss a little more about her, and even memorize one of her prayers, in the next chapter. For now, let's just imagine that bouquet of little flowers at location 19.

The twentieth and twenty-first locations, the center of the dining-room table and the site of the wall thermometer, will require no special mnemonic images right now. For these two great figures represent not ancient history, but recent memory and the present time — as well as the future of the Church. There were many great saints in the twentieth century, and there will be more in this century. But to start the mnemonic framework for these last two centuries, I propose the use of *John Paul II* and *Pope Benedict XVI* themselves. We've been truly blessed to have such profound spiritual leaders during such trying modern times. Who could possible forget them?

TWENTY-ONE CENTURIES OF CHURCH HISTORY

Location	**Image**	**Saint (Doctors in boldface)**
18. Dining-room doorway	*Juniper tree*	Bl. Junipero Serra (1713-1784)
19. Head of table	*Bouquet of little flowers*	**St. Thérèse of Lisieux** (1873-1897)
20. Center of table	*Pope John Paul II*	Pope John Paul II (1920-2005)
21. Thermometer	*Pope Benedict XVII*	Pope Benedict XVI (b. 1927)

We've done it now. We've assembled a framework for twenty-one centuries of church history. Now, anytime you learn of a new great Christian, add him to the appropriate location (century). This framework could be stocked with hundreds or thousands over time. Further, feel free to add important events, doctrinal developments, Church councils, and so on, in their proper order. Of course, events of secular world history could also be added to provide a richer context.

Aristotle and St. Thomas Aquinas both described the human soul as spiritual because it has no material limits. It can hold all things. A memory armed with a framework like this one may not hold *all* things, but it will surely hold *a lot*!

MEMORY MASTER TIPS AND FACTS

QUESTION 23

What's the quickest way to flesh in this mnemonic for Church history?

One way is to try combining the method of loci with mnemonic acronym techniques. (Remember HOMES, EGBDF, and MVEMJSUNP from the foreword?) Let's say, for example, that you recall St. Thomas on the sofa representing the thirteenth century, and you'd like to remember some of the key figures of his day. Just imagine that Thomas is saying "A Red Bird Flies Low" (ARBFL). Picture him pointing at it as it flies right in front of him. *A* would stand for his teacher Albertus Magnus, *R* for his friend Friar Reginald, *B* for his colleague St. Bonaventure, *F* for Emperor Fredric, and *L* for St. Louis, King of France. Get that one down, and you'll know six key figures from the thirteenth century.

Chapter 24

The Twenty-Five Parts of the Cardinal Virtues

"I answer that, Parts are of three kinds, namely, integral, as wall, roof, and foundations are part of a house; subjective, as ox and lion are parts of animal; and potential, as the nutritive and sensitive powers are parts of the soul. Accordingly, parts can be assigned to virtues in three ways."

St. Thomas Aquinas, *Summa Theologica*, II-II, 48

So you didn't know that virtues had parts? St. Thomas was very adept at taking abstract concepts apart and putting them back together again in masterful arrangements. Drawing on classical philosophers such as Aristotle and Cicero, as well as Scripture and the writings of the Church Fathers, St. Thomas described many parts of the cardinal virtues and classified them into three kinds:

- *Integral parts*. The first kind, *integral* parts, are "the conditions for the occurrence of which are necessary for virtue" (*ST*, II-II, 143). In other words, the integral parts are the "must haves" of the virtues. If you lack any one of them, the virtue cannot be fully expressed. St. Thomas describes them as part of the virtues "as wall, roof, and foundation are parts of a house." How appropriate for our house-based mnemonic system! If it's missing any integral part, the cardinal virtue is incomplete. The integral parts of prudence, for example, are *memory*, *understanding*, *docility*, *shrewdness*, *reason*, *foresight*, *circumspection*, and *caution*.

• *Subjective parts*. The second kind are *subjective* parts, "which are its species; and the species of a virtue have to be differentiated according to difference of matter or object" (*ST*, II-II, 143). For example, the subjective parts of prudence refer to the prudence whereby we govern ourselves, and also the prudence whereby we govern others, be it an army or a nation for a select few, or, for most of us, a domestic household.

• *Potential parts*. Finally, we have *potential* parts, which Thomas also calls secondary or annexed virtues. "The potential parts of a virtue are the virtues connected with it, which are directed to certain secondary acts or matters, not having, as it were, the whole power of the principal virtue" (*ST*, II-II, 49, 1). The virtues thus associated with prudence are *euboulia*, *synesis*, and *gnome*. These Greek terms are gleaned from Aristotle and mean, respectively, taking good counsel, forming right judgment in practical matters, and judging from higher principles in special cases.

Let's look at the parts of prudence again, all together:

Integral Parts

Memory Understanding Docility Shrewdness
Reason Foresight Circumspection Caution

Subjective Parts

Governance of self Governance of others

Potential Parts

Eubolia *Synesis* *Gnome*

Drawing from the ethical writings of Aristotle, Cicero, the Bible, and Church Fathers, St. Thomas describes all three kinds of parts of all four cardinal virtues in great depth in the second part of the second part of the *Summa Theologica* (got that?). It's worthwhile reading if you desire to know the cardinal virtues in all their splendor. To keep things more manageable for our purposes, later I'm going to list only those parts of the cardinal virtues that easily lend themselves to contemplation and further study. These will include the eight integral parts of prudence, the nine potential parts of justice, the four integral parts of fortitude, and the four potential parts of temperance, thus yielding twenty-five parts in all.

Knowing these parts by heart can be useful for self-motivation and examination of conscience. In the morning, for example, we can prepare ourselves to try to express and ingrain as habit one or more of the parts that we feel we lack. At night, we can review the parts to examine the extent to which we have worked to live them throughout the day.

Here's my suggestion for memorizing these parts. In chapter 5 we learned the four cardinal virtues, remember? *Prudence*, that three-faced beauty, guided us into the dining room at location 18; the judge representing *justice* sat at the head of the dining-room table at location 19; the fort of *fortitude* stood on the dining-room table at location 20; and the thermometer that reminds us of *temperance* was hanging on the wall at location 21. We already know these, so let's go back to that location and build on from there. With the virtue of prudence I'll demonstrate an extension of the loci technique, and I encourage you to apply it to the remaining cardinal virtues.

So picture Prudence, that three-faced beauty, standing just inside the dining room. Picture her holding a *statue of Mnemosyne*, the Greek goddess of *memory*. The memory goddess statue is nibbling on a *raisin*, for *reason* is the second part of prudence. You look up from the raisin and realize that Prudence is *standing under* a *silly*

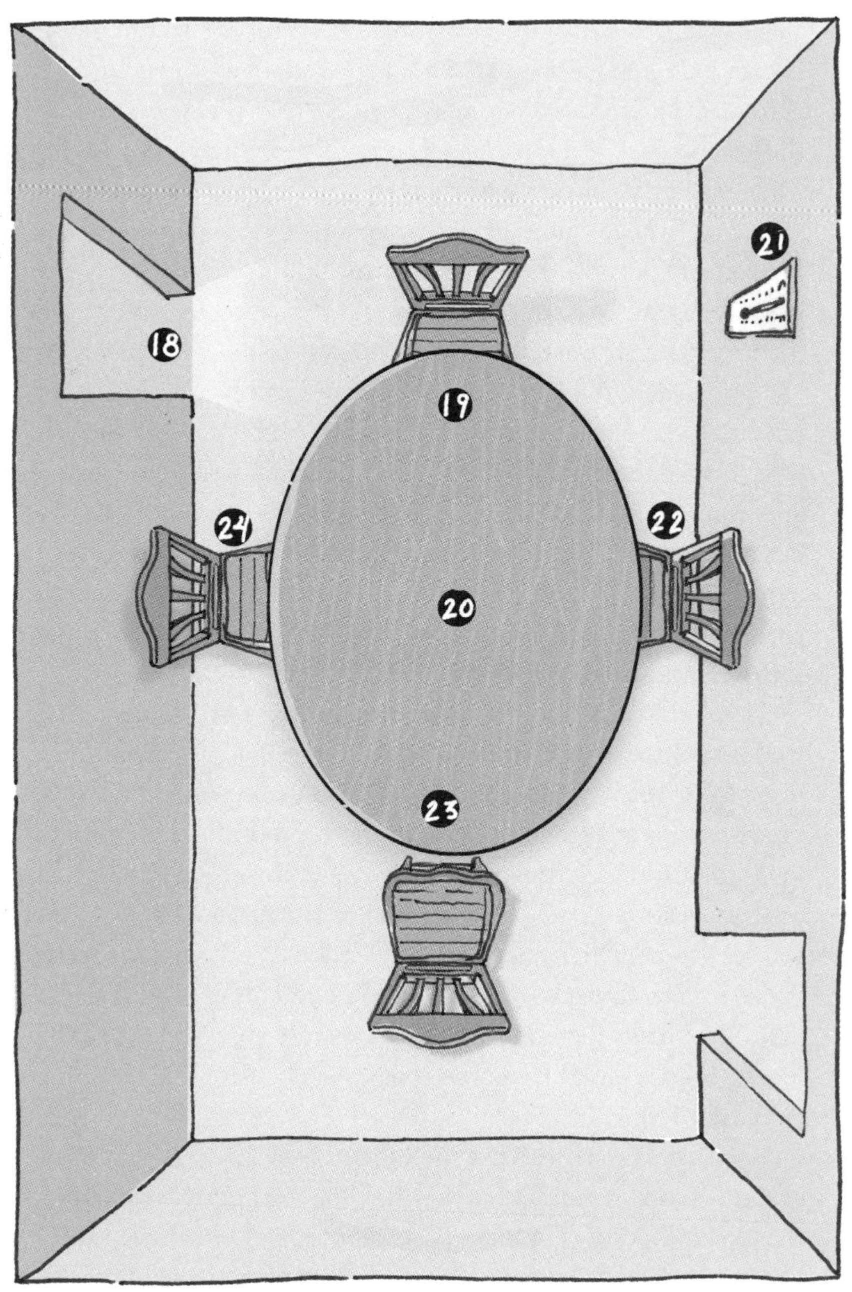

Dining Room

doctor suspended from the ceiling: *understanding* and *docility* are the third and fourth parts. A *shrew* is nibbling on the doctor's coat, reminding us of *shrewdness*. The shrew must have poor vision, since he's wearing glasses *"for sight"* — and to make us think of *foresight*. The shrew starts spinning around in a *circle to see* everything (*circumspection*), and you *caution* him that he's going to make himself sick, thus exercising the eighth and final part of prudence.

THE INTEGRAL PARTS OF PRUDENCE

Part of prudence	**Image**
Memory	*Memory statue*
Reason	*Raisin*
Understanding	*Standing under*
Docility	*Silly doctor*
Shrewdness	*Shrew*
Foresight	*Glasses (for sight)*
Circumspection	*Circling (to see)*
Caution	A *warning of caution*

Here we haven't complicated things by using additional numbers or loci, but, by stringing these images together and connecting each one with the last, I think you'll see that, with a little practice, you can remember them all, in order.

Can you apply the same technique to the parts of justice, fortitude, and temperance? Starting with the image and location already learned for that virtue, build a chain of images to represent each part. If you've mastered the mnemonic house, you should be able to do this. Therefore, for the last three virtues, I'll supply just the parts and leave the labor to you. Since memory is a part of prudence and virtues are the building blocks of good character, we can consider this mnemonic exercise both a memory-building and character-building experience.

THE POTENTIAL PARTS OF JUSTICE

Location	Image	Part
______________	______________	Religion
______________	______________	Piety
______________	______________	Observance
______________	______________	Gratitude
______________	______________	Vindication
______________	______________	Truth
______________	______________	Friendship
______________	______________	Gentleness
______________	______________	Liberality
______________	______________	Equity

Please note well that this chapter illustrates a very important point: the locations we've used for the various lists can serve as a

THE INTEGRAL PARTS OF FORTITUDE

Location	Image	Part
______________	______________	Magnificence
______________	______________	Magnanimity
______________	______________	Patience
______________	______________	Perseverance

THE POTENTIAL PARTS OF TEMPERANCE

Location	Image	Part
______________	______________	Continence
______________	______________	Mildness
______________	______________	Meekness
______________	______________	Modesty

skeleton that we can flesh out to our hearts' content. Once you remember a concept in a given location, you can build additional chains of images for associated information.

This would be most ideal for the Church-history mnemonic from chapter 23. We'll also apply it in the next chapter to expand the family tree of the seven capital sins. And imagine the possible applications once you know the books of the Bible. Just add images for your favorite themes and texts to the proper location. (In chapters 26 and 27, we'll see how to memorize those texts, chapter and verse.)

Practicing the Parts of Prudence

I find the parts of prudence helpful when I'm faced with a difficult life decision. I can ask myself questions like these: "Have I encountered or read about situations like this before? If so, what lessons have I learned?" (memory). "Have I really thought this through logically?" (reason). "Have I really grasped the essence of the situation? What general ethical principles come to bear on this particular situation I'm facing?" (understanding). "Have I been willing to seek the advice of others, including Scripture and other ethical writings?" (docility). "Have I really employed all my wits on this one?" (shrewdness). "Have I tried to imagine the consequences of my actions for myself and for others?" (foresight). "Have I considered all the relevant special circumstances that could affect this decision?" (circumspection). "Have I taken my time to reflect on these issues before acting?" (caution).

A mental review of the parts of each of the cardinal virtues can be useful when we're faced with trying situations that might lead us away from the virtuous path. Feeling weak or fearful? Review the parts of fortitude. Are you tempted? Think about temperance and all its parts.

MEMORY MASTER TIPS AND FACTS

QUESTION 24

What were the three parts of the virtue of prudence according to Marcus Tullius Cicero?

Memory, intelligence, and foresight. "Tully" emphasized that we must be able to draw on past learning and to reason well in the present to plan rightly for the future. St. Thomas drew on the writings of Cicero and other great thinkers to arrive at his more thorough synthesis of the parts of virtues, as we have seen.

Chapter 25

The Forty-Four Daughters of the Capital Sins

"Further, a capital sin is one to which daughters are assigned."

St. Thomas Aquinas, *Summa Theologica*, II-II, 35, 4

If you didn't realize that virtues had parts, chances are you don't know that sins have daughters (unless you were paying close attention during chapter 4, on the capital sins). Remember that the capital sins were considered deadly partly because of the other sins they engender. They lead us down a slippery slope. They set up vicious circles. Church Fathers have called these related sins, metaphorically speaking, their "daughters."

We've done so much with our loci now that I'll leave their memorization to you, if you're so inclined. And even if your mnemonic muscles feel due for a good rest right now, at least take a second look over these sins right now. Can you see how they may arise from each named capital sin?

If you find yourself battling with one of the capital sins in particular, consider memorizing the parts and seeking out St. Thomas's wonderful analyses for further reflection. I've included their locations in the *Summa Theologica* for those who would care to dig deeper.

THE FORTY-FOUR DAUGHTERS OF THE SEVEN CAPITAL SINS

Location	Image	Daughter
Pride (II-II, 133, 5)		
________	________	1. Disobedience
________	________	2. Boastfulness
________	________	3. Hypocrisy
________	________	4. Contention
________	________	5. Obstinacy
________	________	6. Discord
________	________	7. Eccentricity
Avarice (II-II, 118, 7)		
________	________	8. Treachery
________	________	9. Fraud
________	________	10. Falsehood
________	________	11. Perjury
________	________	12. Restlessness
________	________	13. Violence
________	________	14. Insensitivity to mercy
Envy (II-II, 36, 4)		
________	________	15. Hatred
________	________	16. Tale-bearing
________	________	17. Detraction
________	________	18. Joy at another's misfortune
________	________	19. Grief at another's prosperity

THE FORTY-FOUR DAUGHTERS OF THE SEVEN CAPITAL SINS

Location	Image	Daughter
Wrath (II-II, 158, 8)		
________	________	20. Quarreling
________	________	21. Swelling of the mind
________	________	22. Contumely (rude arrogance)
________	________	23. Clamor
________	________	24. Indignation
________	________	25. Blasphemy
Lust (II-II, 153, 5)		
________	________	26. Blindness of mind
________	________	27. Thoughtlessness
________	________	28. Inconstancy
________	________	29. Rashness
________	________	30. Self-love
________	________	31. Hatred of God
________	________	32. Love of the world
________	________	33. Abhorrence and despair of a future world
Gluttony (II-II, 148, 4)		
________	________	34. Unseemly joy
________	________	35. Scurrility
________	________	36. Uncleanness
________	________	37. Loquaciousness
________	________	38. Dullness of mind as regarding understanding

THE FORTY-FOUR DAUGHTERS OF THE SEVEN CAPITAL SINS		
Location	**Image**	**Daughter**
Sloth (II-II, 35, 4)		
__________	__________	39. Malice
__________	__________	40. Spite
__________	__________	41. Faint-heartedness
__________	__________	42. Despair
__________	__________	43. Sluggishness regarding the commandments
__________	__________	44. Wandering of the mind after unlawful things*

*"Those who find no joy in spiritual pleasures have recourse to pleasures of the body."

MEMORY MASTER TIPS AND FACTS

QUESTION 25

What were the three parts of the human soul according to St. Augustine of Hippo?

Memory, understanding, and will. And here's a small sample of Augustine's eloquent description of his own experience of memory (note how it calls to mind our methods):

> I come to the fields and spacious palaces of memory, where are the treasures of innumerable things, brought into it from things of all sorts perceived by the senses. . . . When I enter here, I require instantly what I will to be brought forth, and something instantly comes; others must be longer sought after. . . . Other things come up readily, in unbroken order, as they are called for; those in front make way for the following; and as they make way, they are hidden from sight, ready to come when I will. All which takes place when I recite a thing by heart (*Confessions*, X, 8: cited in Frances Yates's *The Art of Memory*).

Chapter 26

Three More Mnemonic Systems

"Thomas Aquinas was a highly literate man in a highly literate group, yet his contemporaries reserved their greatest praise not for his books but for his memory, for they understood that it was memory which allowed him to weave together his astonishing works."

Mary Carruthers, *The Book of Memory*

If you've followed along thus far, I hope you've seen that the method of loci is a powerful memory tool, and you've filled your house with important Christian tenets (and in chapters 17 and 23, a number of Christian *tenants*). Considering the rich history of the Christian faith, with the sacred Scriptures and the two thousand years of Church history since the time of Christ, surely there's a great deal of other information you'd like to bring home. Perhaps you'd like to be able to recite from memory things like creeds, prayers, psalms, or certain favorite Bible passages. Perhaps you'd like to be able to pick up a little specialized Christian vocabulary in Latin or Greek. Or maybe you'd like to be able to cite some of those favorite Scripture quotations by chapter and verse. Sure, you can add on some imaginary rooms, if you like. And we've already seen that the same rooms can be used again to house different information.

But there are some secret passageways in our house of memory that I haven't mentioned before. These techniques provide special shortcuts to memorize special kinds of material. So, let's open that little door we hadn't noticed before and see where it takes us. (I'll drop the house metaphor now, and we'll get down to business.)

Chapter and Verse:
Converting Numbers to Words

Let's try another variant of visual imagery mnemonics that will allow us to remember where scores of our favorite biblical passages are located by book, chapter, and verse. Do this:

- Imagine that a brilliant red cardinal has just swooped down upon a giant wisdom tooth, but it can't lift the tooth because it's weighed down by a giant fig sitting on top of it.

- Imagine the dome of a state capitol building being lifted by a sinful Titan who says he's just looking for his mom.

- Imagine another giant dried fruit, this time a raisin. It falls on the head of a Roman soldier drinking a glass of tea. A child's toy top floats in the glass, like an ice cube.

- Imagine a most beautiful woman ringing a bell for a charity. She's standing under a giant Greek column. She puts down the bell and begins beating on a tom-tom.

Now, you're probably thinking again of the line "What's this got to do with the price of beans?" Okay, I admit this will take a little explaining. Let's lay out the most important images here.

Cardinal	*Wisdom tooth*	Fig
Capital	*Sinful Titan*	Mom
Raisin	*Roman*	Tea and top
Charity	*Greek column*	Tom-Tom

What have we accomplished? Believe it or not, we've almost locked in book, chapter, and verse for four important Bible verses: one on the cardinal virtues, one relevant to the capital sins, one on the ability of reason to deduce God's existence, and one on the virtue of charity. Please look again at the words in the column on the left. The cardinal represents the cardinal virtues, the capital represents the capital sins, the raisin represents reason, and charity stands for the virtue of charity. We've done this kind of thing before.

Next, look at the second column. The wisdom tooth stands for the book of Wisdom, the Titan stands for Paul's letter to Titus, the Roman for Paul's letter to the Romans, and the single Greek column for his first letter to the Corinthians. Hey, we already used these very same images in the two chapters on the Bible!

Anyway, we have our mnemonic images for the subject matter and the books of the Bible now. But where are the numbers for the chapters and verses? It's in the last column of words that we're breaking new ground: fig, mom, tea and top, and tom-tom. How can this be? Do these images tell us the chapters and verses? They do.

There's a very simple mnemonic system that converts numbers into words. I must admit that I don't know who invented this particular technique, or how long it has been around, but I know firsthand that it definitely works! It's what I used when I memorized the fifty-digit numbers I'd have my students call out. I'd simply convert those fifty meaningless digits into twenty-five meaningful words, turn those words into visual images, and place them in a series of locations I already knew like the back of my hand, or maybe even better. (I rarely look at the back of my hand.)

When I'd give back the numbers, I would just translate them back from the words to the numbers. The code that converts numbers to words is quite easy to remember. I haven't seen it in writing for years, but I'm pretty sure I can reproduce it for us now.

1 = *t* or *d*
2 = *n*
3 = *m*
4 = *r*
5 = *l*
6 = *j*, *sh*, *ch*, *tch*, or soft *g*
7 = *k*, hard *c*, or hard *g*
8 = *f*, *v*, or *ph*
9 = *p* or *b*
0 = *s*, *z*, or soft *c*

I remember the code because I often use it. But the code is also designed to be easily memorized. These tips might help you remember the code until you've locked it in:

T or *d*, like the numeral 1, has one downstroke. The small letter *n* is formed in two strokes, and *m* in three. *R* is the last letter of the word *four*. *L* is the Roman numeral for fifty. The numeral 6 has some resemblance to a backward *j*. Flip the numeral 7 around and add another diagonal, and you'll have a symbol approximating a *K*. The 8 has been likened to an ice-skater's figure eight, and the word *figure* starts with an *f*. Flip around a 9 and you nearly have a *p*. Finally, as for 0, the word *zero* starts with *z*. The other optional letters for some of the numerals represent consonants with similar sounds. They provide more flexibility in producing words for mnemonic images.

This system employs only consonant sounds. The vowel sounds you choose are completely optional. Let's go back to the last column on page 200. Our words were *fig*, *mom*, *tea* and *top*, and *tom-tom*. Let's start with the first scene we imagined. The cardinal was swooping down on a wisdom tooth weighed down by a fig. The first two images remind us that there's a quotation about the cardinal virtues in the book of Wisdom. The last image is the fig, and *it will always be the last of our images that stores the numbers for chapter and verse.* Now let's consider the word *fig*. The consonants are *f* and *g*. Look at the conversion table on page 202. *F* always means the number 8, and *g* always stands for 7. So, if you remember this image and you know the number/letter conversion system, you'll know that the quotation on the cardinal virtues is in the book of Wisdom, chapter 8, verse 7.

As for the other examples, the quotation relevant to the capital sins is in the letter to Titus. The last image was the Titan searching for his mom. The only two consonant sounds in mom are the *m*s, and the conversion table tells us *m* means 3. The verse we're trying to remember must be Titus 3:3.

The next verse, on reason, is in Paul's letter to the Romans. The Roman was drinking tea with a top in it — *tea* and *top*. The word *tea* has only the consonant sound of *t*, and *t*, as we see, means 1. The other word, *top*, starts with a *t* (1) and ends with a *p* (9), so *top* can stand for no other number than 19. The verse in question is Romans 1:19.

Last but not least (in fact, the greatest of all) is charity. This famous verse is in St. Paul's first letter to the Corinthians. Our last image was a tom-tom. Let's look at the conversion chart. *T* means 1, and *m* means 3. This must be 1 Corinthians 13:13. Is this clear? Let's work a couple from the other way around (numbers to words) to be sure.

If we want to recall the number 22, for example, we simply have to come up with some word with two *n* sounds, such as *nun*. If we create the image of a nun, we'll always be able to translate this image back only to the number 22.

How about 97? We could use either a *p* or a *b* sound for the 9 and a *k* or a *g* sound for the 7. Possibilities would include the words *pig*, *puck*, *bag*, *buck*, *pack*, *bug*, or a whole *peck* (that's another one) of other words. It doesn't matter which you use, as long as it makes for a memorable image. They all translate back to 97 and to 97 only.

You can use these for single-digit numbers, like the *tea* we used to represent 1. You could also use them for numbers of three digits or more, 64053, for example (*j*, *r*, *s*, *l*, *m* per our table), could be remembered with the word *Jerusalem*. For most practical purposes, including Bible verses, using the conversion system for only one or two digits at a time should work best.

The four passages above have already been cited in this book, by the way. Do you have some favorite passages you'd like to memorize by chapter and verse? Why not give it a try?

A Secret "Passage" Way

I assume you have some favorite Bible passages that you'd like to know not only by their chapter and verse, but also by heart. This might also be the case for some prayers, creeds, psalms, or songs. This is a relatively simple matter, but *not* an easy one. In this case there's just no way of getting around a good deal of time and effort, whether you employ mnemonics or not. Some of the ancient Roman writers on memory distinguished between "memory for things," which we have really been doing all along, and "memory for words." Sure, all we have been remembering are words that relate to things, but in this case "memory for words" refers to *remembering the exact words of a lengthy passage*. In these cases, I recommend the old-fashioned but tried-and-true system of rote rehearsal to begin with and to continue with, even if mnemonic images are called in to assist.

Let's try one example. In actual practice, I recommend that you first read the text — in this case, a prayer — out loud a few times. But for our purposes of learning the mnemonic aid for the first time (and, yes, to add to the suspense), I'm going to provide the mnemonic images first.

Let's return to the rooms of our house again. Any one of them will work. I'll use the foyer again, our first room, to keep it simple. Here we go.

Imagine that someone is *throwing flowers* at the front door. Do you remember that cursing doormat we met when we were learning the Ten Commandments? Well, the thing is still acting *mean*, but it's *offering you* something. You look out the glass panel, and the *first* thing you see are *fruits*. The portrait on the wall is very tiny. A small girl tells you it's the "*least size*" she has ever seen. Next to the gun rack is a man with a very strong accent. He's chasing a mouse and says, "*Dee pest woes* [the pest was] right here."

In the center of the foyer is a woman with several bottles of dishwashing liquid (the brand is *Joy*, to be exact). She glances back and forth between the bottles and a bunch of sparrows perched on the chandelier. You hear her excitedly praising "*my Joys and my sparrows*." You notice next in the mirror on the wall a reflection of an ancient holy man preparing to slaughter a very small animal for a very *little sacrifice*. Next, on the bench is a very proud *Caesar*, holding a huge bouquet, proclaiming, "*These are my flowers*."

Whew! As I said, this takes a little work. Now, what have we accomplished? Let's look at our locations and our images again:

Location	**Image**
1. Front door	*Throwing flowers*
2. Doormat	*Mean, offering you*
3. Glass panel	*First fruits*
4. Portrait	"*Least size*"
5. Gun rack	"*Dee pest woes*"
6. Center of foyer	"*My Joys*"
7. Chandelier	"*And my sparrows*"
8. Mirror	*Little sacrifice*
9. Bench	*Caesar: "These are my flowers."*

Let's see now what we've actually learned:

Location	**Image**	**Meaning**
1. Front door	*Throwing flowers*	"Throwing flowers
2. Doormat	*Mean, offering you*	means offering you,
3. Glass panel	*First fruits*	as first fruits,
4. Portrait	*"Least size"*	the least sighs,
5. Gun rack	*"Dee pest woes"*	the deepest woes,
6. Center of foyer	*"My Joys"*	my joys
7. Chandelier	*"And my sparrows"*	and my sorrows,
8. Mirror	*Little sacrifice*	my little sacrifices.
9. Bench	*Caesar: "These are my flowers."*	These are my flowers."

Throwing flowers means offering you, as first fruits, the least sighs, the deepest woes, my joys and my sorrows, my little sacrifices. These are my flowers.
St. Thérèse of Lisieux

In this example, we have used the ludicrous to memorize the beautiful — a passage from one of the many simple poems of the nineteenth-century French Carmelite nun and Doctor of the Church whose name you recall from chapter 23. In her short life on earth she provided us with a spiritual legacy that has brought sweetness and joy to millions. I hope you'll forgive the digression, but St. Thérèse, "the Little Flower," is the patron saint of my parish, and it would be a disservice to my readers if I didn't point to her writings as a delightful restorative for minds that might be a bit fatigued from all these mnemonics!

Back to our mnemonics one last time, though. Let me reiterate that my first suggestion for passages such as prayers or creeds or Bible texts is simply to *read and repeat them* the old-fashioned way. In these cases, pull out your mnemonic bag of tricks only if you find that you need them. They might be useful for just a particular difficult line or two. And once you've locked the complete text into your memory, don't worry, the silly images will fade and the beauty of the passage will linger.

Is It All Greek (or Perhaps Latin) to You?

This is the last mnemonic technique in the house (although it doesn't require use of the house). Again, I'm not sure who invented this one. I first saw this referred to as the "keyword method" in the psychological research of the 1970s, but surely some variation has been around as long as man has sought to learn new words.

For our purposes, it can be used to learn new religious terminology, whether in English, in Latin, in Greek, in Hebrew, in Arabic, or in any language, including our own. Here are a few examples using Latin.

Imagine that the Lord is standing with you and you see gigantic *dominoes* drinking *tea* and using a *comb*. Got that one? One Latin phrase from the beautiful hymn *Ave Maria* is "*Dominus tecum*." This comes to mind for me because in the nineteenth-century German composer Anton Bruckner's version of the *Ave Maria*, this phrase is held for quite a stretch for a wonderful effect. But what does *Dominus tecum* mean? Assuming that you're not familiar with the Latin, just think of what comes after "Hail Mary, full of grace" in the prayer (or in Luke 1:28). Yes, it means "the Lord is with you," as in "Hail Mary, full of grace, *the Lord is with thee*." Let's examine what we've done here, one word at a time.

The first Latin word was *Dominus*. It means *lord* (*the* Lord in Church usage.) Since this word might be unfamiliar, we substituted the familiar English word *dominoes* simply because it sounds like *Dominus*. But *Dominus* surely doesn't *mean* dominoes, does it? No. That's why we incorporated the mental image of the Lord. If you imagine both the Lord *and* dominoes, then dominoes serves as the familiar "key word" that helps you lock in the *sound* of the unfamiliar word, and the associated mental image (the Lord) locks in its *meaning*.

Moving along to *tecum*, *te* is one version of the Latin word for *you*, and *cum* is the Latin word for *with*. In this case, the Romans lumped them together as one word, *tecum* ("you with," or as we would arrange it, "with you"). We used the word (and image) of tea as the keyword for *te*, and *comb* as the keyword for *cum* because they have similar sounds. We pictured the Lord standing *with you* to lock in the meaning. (What happened to the *is*?) In some simple Latin statements where the intention is clear, *is* can be omitted, as it has been in Latin renderings of the *Ave Maria*.

Let's try this with a few more simple examples of Latin vocabulary (Latin is the official language of the Church, after all). Let's begin with a line from near the end of the *Ave Maria*: *Ora pro nobis peccatoribus* ("Pray for us sinners").

Latin	**Keyword(s)**	**Image**	**Meaning**
Ora	Oar	*Boat oar praying*	Pray
Pro	Golf pro	*Golf pro yelling "Fore!"*	For
Nobis	No bees	*Someone yelling "No bees on us!"*	Us
Peccatoribus	Pec tore a bus	*A massive chest muscle*	Sinners

Now, I'm *not* suggesting that you go through prayers in foreign languages and learn them word-by-painstaking-word this way. What I'd like you to know is that you can apply the keyword technique to new words in *any* language, including unfamiliar words in your own language. The key word captures at least some of the sound, to help with the pronunciation. The associated image locks in the meaning.

Here's one last simple example, this time from French, to make sure that we have the keyword method down. Suppose you simply want to remember that the French word for *book* is *livre* (pronounced something like "leev-reh"). Picture a tree with *books* instead of *leaves*. *Leaves* is the keyword for the sound, and the books form the associated image locking in the meaning. Any questions? (If there are, you can look up more information on techniques such as this in a good memory *livre* like Harry Lorayne and Jerry Lucas's *The Memory Book*.)

It's time to leave these the passageways and return to the rooms of the house, armed with the additional mnemonic tools we've just added to our tool belts.

MEMORY MASTER TIPS AND FACTS

QUESTION 26

Can mnemonics handle the multiple forms of Greek and Latin words?

Languages such as Greek and Latin are "inflected." There are many possible forms for most nouns, verbs, and adjectives. *Deus* for example, means "God" in Latin; but *Dei* means "of God"; *Deo* means "to God" or "for God"; *Deum* means God as the object of an action; and *Deo* may also mean "with God" or "by God." But there are a limited number of forms these words may take. Nouns, for example, fall into five main patterns called declensions. *Deus* is a second-declension masculine noun; it always starts with *De* but has differing endings — namely, *-us*, *-i*, *-o*, *-um*, and *-o* again. Those endings will show up on scads of other second-declension masculine and neuter nouns, so they're a must for memorization, if you want to master Latin.

Here's what I do. I convert the *-us*, *-i*, *-o*, *-um*, *-o*, into a phrase and mnemonic image based on an approximation of their sounds. I picture a small Roman child showing his mother a delicious piece of O-shaped cereal: "You see O, yum O?" Using images combining sounds and pictures like this one, I've placed all five Latin noun declensions on a statue of Augustus Caesar in my study. If you really take to these mnemonic systems, you can exercise your creativity to modify and combine them to handle all kinds of complicated material. You might even come to say, like Julius Caesar, "*Veni, vidi, vici!*" ("I came, I saw, I conquered!")

Chapter 27

Twelve Red-Letter Sayings of Jesus Christ

"Man shall not live by bread alone, but by every word that proceeds from the mouth of God."

Matthew 4:4

Why "red letter"? Haven't you seen the beautiful editions of the Bible that print all of Jesus' own words in red ink? The twelve direct quotations in this list are but a tiny small sample of the wonderful, loving statements Jesus shared with us. I hope readers will apply this technique to recall other passages that speak especially to their souls. And, oh yes, we won't need any red ink. We'll highlight these passages with mnemonics.

Our mnemonic focus here is to remember the exact locations of these verses in the Gospels (chapter and verse). For each verse:

- Place the evangelist in the locations of the foyer that we used in the New Testament chapter.
- Imagine a key word or two from the *saying*.
- Pair it with the *evangelist*.
- Add images that stand for the *chapter and verse* using the number/letter conversion system described in the last

chapter. (To keep the content and the chapter/verse images clear, make the chapter/verse image *an exclamation — something being said*, by the evangelist, Jesus, or someone with them. You'll see what I mean in just a minute.)

Here are the verses:

MATTHEW (4:4, 6:9, 7:12)

"Man shall not live by bread alone, but by every word that proceeds from the mouth of God."

"Pray, then, like this: Our Father who art in heaven, hallowed by thy name. . . ."

"So whatever you wish that men would do to you, do so to them; for this is the law and the prophets."

MARK (8:36, 12:17, 14:22)

"For what does it profit a man to gain the whole world and forfeit his life?"

"Render to Caesar the things that are Caesar's, and to God the things that are God's."

"And as they were eating, he took bread, and blessed and broke it, and said, 'Take; this is my body.' "

LUKE (6:41; 9:23; 18:16)

"Why do you see the speck that is in your brother's eye, but do not notice the log that is in your own eye?"

"If any man would come after me, let him deny himself and take up his cross daily and follow me."

"Let the children come to me, and do not hinder them; for to such belongs the kingdom of God."

JOHN (3:16, 6:51, 8:31-32)
"For God so loved the world that he gave
his only Son, that whoever believes in him
should not perish but have everlasting life."

"I am the living bread which came down from heaven;
if anyone eats of this bread, he will live forever;
and the bread which I shall give for
the life of the world is my flesh."

"If you continue in my word, you are truly
my disciples, and you will know the truth,
and the truth will make you free."[4]

Matthew

For the first verse, we could picture at the front door a lone loaf of bread being held by Matthew as he explains the word of God to an old man who is hard of hearing. The man tells Matthew to *"roar!"* his message to him. The two *r*s in *roar* each represent a 4. There we have Matthew 4:4.

These passages are so striking and memorable that it probably won't take more than simple attentive repetition to remember the actual words. If you have difficulty with any, though, feel free to try out the memory-for-words technique in chapter 26.

Since this mnemonic is rather complicated, let's walk through the rest of the dozen sample sayings (all containing words well worth remembering). Next, still at the front door, because this is the location we've assigned to Matthew, we imagine that Matthew is kneeling to say the Our Father when he's amazed to see an Old Testament figure appear before his eyes. He calls out, *"Job!"*

[4] Of relevance to our house mnemonic, note that in some translations "continue in my word" reads "make my word your home."

The Lord's Prayer reminds us that this is the passage where Jesus teaches us this prayer. Matthew's exclamation *"Job!"* is the key to the chapter and verse, since the *j* translates only to a 6, and the *b* translates only to a 9 — must be Matthew 6:9.

Next, imagine Matthew (still at the front door, of course) picking up a golden ruler. This tells us this passage is where Jesus introduces the Golden Rule, of course. Imagine that Matthew says, "Go, tin!" implying that other rules of conduct are as base metal compared with this one. Check out the numerical conversion for "Go, tin!" (I've provided all of the numerical conversions for these verses in a table on page 216), and you'll know the Golden Rule's exact location is Matthew 7:12. I'll go through the rest of these verses in short order. Remember that the table that follows will fill in the number/letter conversions (and the complete number/letter conversion table appears in chapter 26).

Mark

We're now at Mark's location on the doormat in the foyer. Imagine Mark looking at a dead man on the ground, his hands still clutching a sack of gold. Imagine Mark with Eve. (Yes, we're jumping around in time a bit, pairing Mark with Eve, but this is no problem in the world of imagery mnemonics!) It's dark outside, so as Mark crouches down, he says, "Eve, match!" (8:36). Next, see Mark talking to Caesar himself, in all his toga-clad splendor. One of Caesar's dogs growls at Mark, and Caesar is kind enough to say "Down, dog!" (which translates to 12:7). Finally, Mark holds aloft a loaf of bread shaped like a body and, seeing the face of a dear friend wearing a habit, he calls out, "Dear nun!" (14:22).

Luke

Through the glass panel by the front door, we see Luke out in the front yard. Unfortunately, he has a large log in his eye, so he's asking his friend Joe to read to him: "Joe, read!" This translates to

6:41. Next you notice that the log in Luke's eye has changed into a cross. His friend Joe advises him to "Be numb!" (9:23) to endure the pain of carrying it. Lastly, see Luke surrounded by children. He's gathering them into a pickup truck to take them to Jesus. One of the kids says, "Tuff Dodge!" (which must translate to Luke 18:16).

John

A painting of John hangs on the foyer wall. It includes God the Father showing the Son the pickup truck that John had lent to Luke. Elated that they're present near his own truck, John cries out, "My Dodge!" (Granted, some of these scenes are quite unlikely, but I have to make things work with whatever the chapter and verse numbers happen to be. With more practice, I'm sure you'll be able to come up with some more elegant images!) "My Dodge!" translates to 3:16.

Now John sees bread falling from the heavens. This is very special bread, of course. Imagine that rays of light shine forth from it, like the Eucharist displayed in a golden monstrance. John says "Gee, light!" so we'll remember this verse as John 6:51. Last of all, we imagine John in chains (not entirely an uncommon experience for the early Christians). Imagine that he finds a "true key," representing the truth that will set him free. John says, "Have might, man!" to himself, as he turns the iron key within the massive, rusty lock (8:31-32).

There you have them. Twelve profound Scripture passages, serving as examples of one of the most demanding mnemonic systems. This system can be most useful (and not nearly so demanding), when used not for twelve passages at once, but for the occasional single verse that really moves you or is especially important to remember. Locking in one verse at a time this way is no great effort, and it provides practice with the number/letter conversion

TWELVE RED-LETTER SAYINGS OF JESUS CHRIST

Content image	Number/letter conversion image	Verse(s)
Matthew holds bread and Gospel	"*Roar!*" (r, r = 4, 4)	Matthew 4:4
Matthew starts the Our Father	"*Job!*" (j, b = 6, 9)	Matthew 6:9
Matthew points to golden ruler	"Go, *tin!*" (g, t, n = 7, 1, 2)	Matthew 7:12
Mark and a dead man	"*Eve, match!*" (v, m, tch = 8, 3, 6)	Mark 8:36
Mark talks to Caesar	"*Down, dog!" (d, n, d, g = 1, 2, 1, 7)*	Mark 12:17
Mark eats bread shaped like body	"*Dear nun!*" (d, r, n, n, = 1, 4, 2, 2)	Mark 14:22
Luke with a log in his eye	"*Joe, read!*" (j, r, d = 6, 4, 1)	Luke 6:41
Luke's log becomes a cross	"*Be numb!*" (b, n, m = 9, 2, 3)	Luke 9:23
Luke calls for children	"*Tuff Dodge!*" (t, f, d, g* = 1, 8, 1, 6)	Luke 18:16
John with the Father and Son	"*My Dodge!*" (m, d, g = 3, 1, 6)	John 3:16
John sees falling bread	"Gee, *light!*" (g, l, t = 6, 5, 1)	John 6:51
John in chains finds true key	"*Have might, man!*" (v, m, t, m, n = 8, 3, 1, 3, 2)	John 8:31-32

*Recall that the hard *g* sound is 7 and soft *g* sound is 6.

code. If this is something you'd like to pursue, consider memorizing one Gospel verse, by chapter and verse, from the reading each Sunday at Mass.

And please note well, if you've mastered the locations for the books of the Old and New Testaments, you already have a built-in framework for remembering the location of any Bible verse you'd like. Hear a good one from the book of *Jeremiah*? Just place it on the pool table. With time, your mnemonic house of the Bible could be very well appointed with beautiful scriptural furnishings.

MEMORY MASTER TIPS AND FACTS

QUESTION 27

Have any great Catholic teachers since Aquinas championed the art of memory?

Matteo Ricci was a Jesuit priest who traveled to China in the sixteenth century to spread the word of Christ. He sought to capture the attention of learned Confucian scholars with modern Western marvels such as maps of the world, mechanical clocks, and prisms. But more relevant for us, he also sought to impress them with something he gleaned from his classical Catholic education: the writings of Albertus Magnus and Thomas Aquinas on artificial memory. The Chinese had long had an elaborate system of rigorous examinations required to obtain lucrative government jobs. Father Ricci figured they would be ripe to learn about artificial memory (which he would also use to introduce Christian themes), and he combined the method of loci with the acronym technique, as I showed you in the chapter on Church history.

Part 5

Remember What I Preach

Chapter 28

Applications for All Ages

"Nothing that you have seen or heard is useful, however, unless you deposit what you should see and hear in the treasury of your memory."

St. Jerome, in Mary Carruthers's *Book of Memory*

I think St. Jerome would agree that by this point we have built up a pretty substantial treasury in our memories. But the trained memory is also a great treasure in itself. It can be used to acquire so many good things. In this chapter, I'll suggest a few places where the treasures of artificial memory might be well spent, and I'll provide some spending tips for fledgling memory masters of almost all ages.

Catechesis

Mnemonic techniques have obvious catechetical potential. The intention of this book has of course been catechetical in the general sense of teaching some basics of the Faith. But these techniques could further be used to supplement formal programs of religious instruction. Any material a catechumen desires to learn by heart can be aided with mnemonic techniques, so I'm going to include some specific suggestions here and in the next chapter for those who teach the Faith to children or adults, with a special emphasis on developmental concerns and the mnemonic strengths and weaknesses of children.

When I examined the formal scientific research on normal memory development and on mnemonic training with children and adolescents, I argued that sixth-graders, children of about eleven or twelve years of age, might be the ideal group for training in mnemonic techniques. Why? Essentially because they're old enough to possess the natural memory and abstract thinking capacities to employ the mnemonic systems, and probably young enough not to have devised much in the way of less effective, hit-and-miss mnemonic strategies of their own. This isn't to say that this system can't be employed with younger children. It can — just with additional work and guidance from a teacher. Older adolescents and adults, if they're not resistant to the idea of mnemonic systems, will be able to use them best, because of their more fully developed cognitive powers and vocabularies.

Here are a few suggestions to help learners with mnemonic systems by age group or school grades:

Elementary-School Students

Visual-imagery mnemonic systems can be used with these children with some very important caveats in mind. Do you remember the "seven plus or minus two" chunks of information most adults can hold in short-term memory? Well, this takes a little time to develop. Before the age of eleven or twelve or so, elementary students will have more limited short-term capacity, and might do best with shorter lists, even when using mnemonics. Further, they'll require more external guidance. Younger children will have greater difficulty understanding how to generate appropriate images, and they will have smaller vocabularies to work with. The teacher should supply them with images and make them as concrete and visually striking as possible. Showing the children drawings depicting not only locations, but also actual mnemonic images, is recommended. (Better yet, have children produce their own drawings in full color.)

Middle-Schoolers, High-Schoolers, and Young Adults

Most middle-schoolers should have the capacity to employ the imagery systems in this book. Older students should be able to use them even more effectively because their larger vocabularies will give them more to pull from when they form their own associative images for material to be remembered. Young adults will be at their absolute prime in terms of raw memory capacities. When I've done classroom presentations of the method of loci with twenty-item lists, invariably more than half of my college students were able to recall all twenty items.

Perhaps the biggest obstacle with these youths is their skepticism about mnemonic systems. Respect for the power of memory is not a hallmark of modern education. And aren't mnemonics just "tricks" or "gimmicks"? Isn't *understanding* what we're seeking, after all? Well, as I said in the introduction, it's hard to understand what you can't remember! The surest cure for the doubting Thomases of mnemonics is to show them what they themselves can do with them.

Seniors

Older Americans are worried about their memory abilities. I saw this first-hand when I tested hundreds of seniors during my doctoral practicum, internship, and dissertation research. Are their concerns justified? Well, there's bad news and good news here. For the minority of older adults who are suffering from a dementing brain disease, mnemonic techniques will be of little use. But for the great majority of older adults in reasonably good health, memory declines tend to be quite modest, and in fact, their mastery of vocabulary might continue to improve as they grow older. When I was doing daily testing of older adults on a three-hour battery of memory tests, in one test I would read a fifteen-word list and ask subjects to repeat as many as they could. This would be repeated for eight trials, to measure how their recall improved with repetition. After dozens of subjects, the first one to give me back all fifteen in the exact order in which I had read them was an 89-year-old Ursuline nun!

The memory abilities of the elderly are characterized by huge individual differences. Some will show noticeable impairment, and some will not. Elderly individuals who try these mnemonics and find that they work might receive a welcome boost in self-confidence. And bear in mind, study after study (including a new one brought to my attention by a colleague this very day) shows that individuals who stay mentally active throughout their adult lives are most likely to hold on to their mental abilities as they age. Use it or lose it!

Apologetics

Here's an area of possible application suggested to me by my barber of almost thirty years. (Thanks, Larry.) Have you ever been asked difficult, critical questions about doctrines of the Catholic Church, or about Christianity in general, and wished you could produce an articulate response off the top of your head? Here's a way you can call mnemonics to your aid. The same handful of criticisms of Catholic doctrine tend to come up again and again. Go to a good book on apologetics, and look at the table of contents. There you'll find topics such as doctrines on Mary, the saints, the papacy, the Bible, and Tradition. You can use a book like that to build your own mnemonic system of Bible-based apologetics.

Form a system of loci with a major topic, such as Marian doctrine, in each location. Then, using the number/letter conversion system presented two chapters ago (and practiced in the last chapter on the sayings of Jesus), add two or three or four specific Bible verses or other sources that provide the origins of the doctrines. The more you learn about these topics, the richer your apologetic loci will become, and the more adept you'll be at providing the reasons for your faith. And you'll do so, of course, not in the spirit of confrontation or biblical one-upmanship, but in the spirit of sharing your faith in a respectful, intelligent manner.

Listen to the Father of Logic on the usefulness of an organized memory when presenting a position:

> For just as in a person with a trained memory, a memory of things themselves is immediately caused by the mere mention of their "places," so these habits too will make a man readier in reasoning, because he has his premises classified before his mind's eye, each under its number (Aristotle, *Topics*, Book VIII).

And let's not overlook St. Peter's advice: "Always be ready to give a defense to everyone who asks you a reason for the hope that is in you" (1 Pet. 3:15).

Academics in General/Homeschooling in Particular

The mnemonic techniques laid out in this book can be applied to virtually any academic material — history, biology, psychology, foreign language learning, you name it — and many psychological research studies back up my claim. You might even have a head start in world history. As we saw in the last chapter, if you know the twenty-one representative figures in the history of the Church, you can add any secular figures or events of your choosing to any of the centuries.

And believe me, these techniques can help take you far beyond fourth-grade geography class. They served me well during my psychology licensing examination. Even a doctoral degree doesn't spare a psychologist from taking a national two-hundred-item objective test demanding good, old-fashioned factual knowledge, complete with right and wrong answers. In fact, an entire industry has developed around preparing for this test, but I skipped the special seminars and put mnemonics to work. (How'd I do? Well, I got the highest score in the state — not only for that year but for a five-year period.) Please remember, though, that mnemonics do not replace study and hard work; they supplement and enhance them.

Perhaps you (or a loved one) will find that mnemonics can help you become licensed or certified in your own field someday. Come to think of it, perhaps you have a young person in your home with the SAT, ACT, GRE, or some other such standardized test looming on the horizon. Since these tests are so important to college applications, massive industries exist to prepare students for tests such as these, offering thorough — and often quite expensive — study programs. Mnemonic techniques can be a very powerful tool to enhance and maximize the value of such formal prep programs.

Indeed, I've had my own college students inform me that mnemonic techniques have helped them on standardized tests. I remember one young lady who told me with no small delight that the mnemonic I'd shown the class for remembering the stages and ages of the developmental theory of psychologist Jean Piaget had also "worked" for her on the GRE.

Mnemonic systems such as these could spell out a huge advantage for homeschooled students, since their peers are not learning these systems in the classroom — not even in Catholic classrooms. (This is unfortunate, because the patron saint of Catholic schools, after all, is none other than St. Thomas Aquinas himself.) Please see the next chapter for some very detailed suggestions for homeschoolers.

A slight warning is in order, though. Students who have mastered imagery mnemonics might feel as if they're cheating on tests, since they'll be "looking at" their notes. But the teacher shouldn't have a problem with this, since those notes will be written in the students' minds!

Public Speaking

I will end where the method of loci began. It was ancient orators who brought us this system. Remember the Greek Simonides? And who was the greatest of Roman orators? Yes, Cicero, who was also one of St. Thomas's ancient sources on the use of "artificial memory" (and on the cardinal virtues). You'd have to be extremely skilled in public speaking to effectively read a speech from a completely written text, or to effectively deliver a speech that was completely memorized, word for word. The sense of spontaneity and of connection with the audience would be so much harder to obtain.

Remember what the ancients did. They'd place a mental image of each important topic in a specific location, making sure they wouldn't forget anything essential, but leaving them free to speak naturally. With the outline of their speech locked in a system of loci (perhaps based on the very forum in which they spoke), they could deliver a detailed, coherent oration in logical order, seemingly without effort. Indeed, the very word *topic* derives from the Greek *topos* ("location"). Further, have you ever heard anyone argue, "Well, in the first *place?*" Yes, it appears that the arts of public speaking and persuasion have strong roots in mnemonic soil. And there's no reason why modern teachers and preachers couldn't grow their lectures or homilies from similarly rich earth.

When teaching lifespan developmental psychology, I kept a tradition of giving the last three-and-a-half-hour lecture of the term (on aging and dying) entirely without notes. The students were usually quite receptive (perhaps hoping I'd soon run out of things to say). As for me, I enjoyed teaching that way, and my lecture *from* memory soon came to rival my lecture *about* memory as my personal favorite.

MEMORY MASTER TIPS AND FACTS

QUESTION 28

Where can I go for more information on artificial memory systems?

Go to Frances Yates's *The Art of Memory* and Mary Carruthers's *The Book of Memory* for exceptionally detailed and enthralling historical accounts of artificial memory. Go to Harry Lorayne and Jerry Lucas's *The Memory Book* for a practical guide with all kinds of interesting techniques (although the method of loci is not emphasized). I first encountered the method of loci in a book discarded by my local library. It contained a set of twenty loci based on the parts of a car, of all things, and I've been "driving" that car for over twenty-five years now! The book is called *Your Memory — Speedway to Success in Earning, Learning, and Living*, by O. W. Hayes.

Chapter 29

How to Teach This System to Your Children

"Train up a child in the way he should go:
and when he is old, he will not depart from it."
Proverbs 22:6

In the last chapter I addressed a few of the areas in which memory systems can be applied, and I included a few practical suggestions here and there. In this chapter you'll find more practical advice, with a specific focus on how adults can teach this system to children. This topic should be of interest to any parent or grandparent who would like to pass along the methods of memory mastery, and I suspect it will be of particular interest to parents who homeschool their children. So, later in this chapter I'll gear a few suggestions specifically to the homeschooling parent, with examples of techniques I've employed in the classroom. But let me begin by sharing a little taste of the formal research findings on memory strategy training with school-age children.

Quite a body of research has accrued on the use of mnemonic techniques by children. Study after study had shown that these techniques can be successfully taught to children of various ages in controlled experiments. Indeed, younger children trained in these techniques often outperform not only peers of their age, but also older students who went without mnemonic training. One study, for example, found that second-graders (seven- and eight-year-olds) provided with mnemonic imagery keywords for new Spanish words outperformed control groups of sixth-graders four years their senior. Another found that fifth- and sixth-graders using keyword images they generated themselves for city-product pairings (i.e., which cities produced which specific goods) were able to outperform control groups of high school juniors and seniors. Several studies have shown that fifth- and sixth-graders who were taught mnemonic techniques sometimes outperform control subjects of the same age by 100 percent or more (i.e., they remember twice as much). Similar findings also hold into the college years. In fact, the favorite experimental group for university psychologists has always been their own students, and study after study has shown that traditional college students from age eighteen to their early twenties also profit from mnemonic training.

I mentioned in the last chapter why I consider age eleven or twelve to be for most children the ideal age for instruction. At this age, their natural short-term memory capacities are near adult capacity, and they're less likely to have developed their own idiosyncratic systems for memory, which are probably not as effective or widely applicable as these tried-and-true imagery and loci mnemonics. Further, their vocabulary and general knowledge base should be developed enough to come up with some of their own mnemonic keywords and images. This isn't to say that elements of this system couldn't be explained to even younger children, but many might lack the ability to understand and apply them fully.

Memory Research from Russia

I'd like to continue with a little bit of theory, and then move on to a dozen suggestions for practical application. As for the theory, let's consider a couple of quotations from the renowned Russian developmental psychologist Lev Vygotsky (1896-1934). The first:

"For the young child, to think means to recall, but for the adolescent, to recall means to think" (*Mind in Society*).

Vygotsky, like Aristotle and St. Thomas Aquinas, was interested in making the most of the potential of the human mind, and mnemonics was one of his many areas of interest. Vygotsky also had a special interest in understanding how the mind grows and develops as we mature from childhood to adulthood. He believed that early adolescence was a crucial time for the blossoming of our full potential for memory. Note that for the child, "to think means to recall." In other words, there isn't a great deal of reflection going on in a young child. When required to think about a problem, he's likely to try to remember what an adult has told him. But for the adolescent, "to recall means to think." Now the ability to reflect and ponder is in bloom.

I haven't mentioned yet that *mnemonics* derives from the ancient Greek word *mnemon*, meaning "mindful, remembering, unforgetting." Not only will the adolescent's thinking be more than a parroting of what he has learned from others, but, for him, even acts of memory can be guided by deliberate, "mindful," strategic thinking. But what can we, as parents or teachers, do to guide the adolescent's thinking toward useful mnemonic techniques? Let's consider another passage from Vygotsky:

> Every function in the child's development appears twice: first on the social level; first between people (interpsychological) and then inside the child (intrapsychological). This applies equally to voluntary attention, to logical memory, and to the formation of concepts. All the higher functions originate as actual relations between human individuals (*Mind in Society*).

Whereas natural memory abilities, such as the "seven plus or minus two" capacity of short-term memory, develop according to nature's timetable, "higher functions," such as artificial memory capacities, develop by way of social influences. This means that concerned adults can play a meaningful role in teaching mnemonics to children. Next, I'll present a dozen suggestions on how you, as a parent, a grandparent, a teacher, or another concerned adult, can use your influence to help a child use this book. Pick and choose any suggestions that appeal to you. I'll assume that the children are at least ten years of age. (And, oh yes, breathe a sigh of relief. Here's a list that you don't have to memorize.)

• *Demonstrate the method of loci.* Children might well be resistant to the idea of using techniques such as these. They might not understand them, might think they won't work, or might complain that they take even more work than rote memory (maybe you thought the same thing yourself). What better way to address those concerns than to show your kids, rather painlessly, that they indeed can use mnemonics? You could do this by slowly and carefully reading them the introductory material on the Ten Commandments. First, show the child the picture of the foyer only, and tell him which images to imagine in which places. Repeat as necessary until he can name all ten images when looking at the picture, and then show him how each image stands for a commandment. Once he grasps the connection, he'll know the Ten Commandments, just as you now do.

• *Show your child that it works.* As an alternative that might prove simpler for the child, but would require more mnemonic expertise of the adult, consider this demonstration. Ask the child to write down ten nouns of his choosing, numbering them in the process. Have the child slowly read them out to you without letting you see the paper. Place images for those nouns in the loci of the foyer as they're called out one by one, and then call them back to the child. You could add to the effect by calling them off backward, last item to first. You could also have the child call out a number from one to ten and then you supply the word; or have the child call out any word and you supply the number. If this gets the child's attention, you could start to explain the loci and image system and let the child try with a list of simple, concrete nouns that you compose.

• *Create a mnemonic room with your child.* Sit with the child in your living room or kitchen or bedroom, and go around the room in order, and both of you decide together on ten places. Ask the child for a list of information he might be interested in learning, and place them in the locations in the room in which you're sitting. (I did this with my children years ago. If I remember correctly, a *washing* machine that weighed a *ton* was coming through our kitchen door, Lurch of the *Addams Family* was sitting on the kitchen table, and somebody's *son* named *Jeff* was knocking on the side door. (Can you tell that we were memorizing the U.S. presidents?) Many children will enjoy the process of letting their imaginations run wild in creating mnemonic images.

• *Read and memorize the items from one chapter or part of one chapter of this book with your child a few nights per week.* Do the mnemonic work together and help each other practice. Quiz each other in spare moments — during the drive to school or while waiting in the orthodontist's office. It might be a while before you can tackle all twenty mysteries of the Rosary or all forty-six books of the Old Testament, but those can be broken up — the Rosary into four sets of five mysteries, and the Old Testament books by the rooms of the mnemonic house.

• *Ask your child to read the foreword to young readers, or read it together.* See if there are questions. Talk over the four basic concepts of organization, imagination, concentration, and repetition. (I still can't guarantee that he'll clean his room, though.)

• *Set memory goals with your child,* and keep them realistic, considering the child's age and natural memory abilities. Of course, there will be individual differences in the ability of children to use these techniques. They might be hard for some, and for others, they may prove fun and easy. Some will bear thirty-fold fruit, some sixty, and some a hundred, we might say.

• *Focus primarily on the method of loci with the rooms of the mnemonic house*, or your own house, at least early on. The techniques for passage retention (memory for words) and number/letter conversion (chapters 26 and 27) are much more advanced.

• *Find some list of information in one of the child's school books and demonstrate how to memorize it with the method of loci.*

• *Practice the material in one of the chapters with other family members or friends*. Do you ever have "family nights"? One evening, instead of playing a board game, you could decide on an impressive-sounding memory challenge for the whole family; the forty-six books of the Old Testament, the twenty-seven books of the New Testament, or those forty-four daughters of the capital sins would be good possibilities. If you have reference materials on hand, you could also work on the Church-history mnemonic as a family. Assign everyone a certain number of saints, Doctors, or popes, or a certain group of centuries, and see if the family collectively can remember a twenty-one-century history with fifty or sixty great personages.

Remember, the Church-history mnemonic could be built up to huge proportions over time, and it could also serve as a segue to some very profound discussions. If a child expresses particular interest in any great saint, buy or borrow a copy of that saint's biography for him. Each saint, of course, will be known for the particular way in which he has lived the Faith. Discuss this with the child. Did this saint especially embody one or more of the virtues or Beatitudes? Did he show a special devotion to the Bible, or to the sacraments, or to Mary?

Children need heroes to inspire them to make the most of their own gifts. One of my sons was quite moved recently when I told him the story of Maximilian Kolbe, the priest who volunteered to be starved to death in a Nazi concentration camp in order to spare the life of a condemned man who had a family. Unfortunately, few of the role models promoted in our popular culture today achieved their fame through their virtue or sanctity.

So try to imagine ways in which these mnemonic exercises can serve as a springboard to fruitful family discussions. Doing these activities as a family offers an opportune time to discuss the meaning and importance of the materials in these lists of the elements of the Faith. If family members have an artistic bent, why not record your mnemonic night's work on a poster board, complete with the list of contents, and some drawings of the actual contents or your mnemonic images?

• *Try to use the information in this book to instill both curiosity about the Catholic Faith and respect for the potential of the mind in your child.* Search for a metaphorical image that speaks to your child. I like to compare training your mind to training your muscles, because of my interest in weightlifting.

When one of my sons recently reached the early teen years, he and his friends became enthralled with fast cars. Here they were, suddenly talking about 427-cubic-inch engines generating 435 horsepower! What a nice opportunity for some metaphorical imagery. Now when we talk about learning and studying, I ask him how he has been using his "engine" (that is, his mind), whether he's just coasting or making the engine roar ("pedal to the metal"), and whether he has been feeding his engine high-octane fuel (good books). I don't want him to settle for a little four-cylinder and end up realizing years later, "I could have had a V-8!"

And come to think of it, maybe he'd be receptive to a souped-up version of the car-part mnemonic now. Can you think of a metaphor for the mind that might appeal to the young learner in your life?

• *Show this book to older adolescents and young adults too*. It was in my late teens that I discovered the world of mnemonics by chance, at a library book sale, and it definitely made my college and post-graduate days much easier.

• *Let your own steadfastness serve as an example*. If you would have your children memorize important information pertaining to the Faith, show them the way by your example. Memorize some lists yourself, acquire some expertise with the method of loci, but most important, show them that this is but a first step. Let them see you reading more books that take you deeper into the mysteries of Catholicism. Show them your hope. Share with them your charity.

The House of Memory in the Homeschool

Perhaps it would be of help to homeschooling parents if I were to explain just how I've demonstrated the method of loci in formal educational settings. Please imagine the following scene.

It's snowing outside, but inside a cozy classroom, thirty college students are shifting around in their chairs, settling in for a nap on this cold winter's night. But alas, their professor has asked for their full attention, so they sit bolt upright, curious to see what he's got in mind.

I typically introduce artificial memory to my students during my lecture on memory development. Later on I'll provide all kinds of material on memory and metamemory, but I start by having the students exercise their own memory capacities. I first ask them to pay attention while I read aloud a list of fifteen words. When I've finished reading the words, I ask the students to write down all the words they can remember, then put the paper away. Next I read the fifteen words again, and ask the students again to write down as many as they can remember on a new piece of paper. Then I display a very complex geometrical figure on the screen. After letting them examine it for a bit, I turn off the projector and ask them to copy as much of it as they can recall. Finally, I ask them a third time to write down as many of the fifteen words as they can remember. When they've finished, I record with tally marks on the blackboard how many words each student remembered on the first and second trials, as well as the third time after the delay.

What does this exercise accomplish? For one thing, it introduces several memory concepts I'll discuss during the lecture, including verbal memory, visual memory, short-term memory, the learning curve, and secondary or long-term memory (retention of information after a delay). I also ask the students what techniques they used to remember the words and the image, which introduces the topics of encoding, storage, retrieval, memory strategies, and metamemory as well. The exercise also gives the students a feel for the capacities of their own short-term memories (and sets them up to be impressed once they see what they can do when I show them the method of loci). How do I demonstrate the method of loci? Good question.

Near the end of the part of the lecture on memory strategies, I introduce my students to the twenty-location system of loci using the parts of a car. I project the image with numbered parts on a screen and explain how the first location is the hood ornament, the second location is the headlights, and so forth, through all the twenty parts of the car. (In this book, of course, we've settled into a sixty-loci house!)

Next, I introduce twenty words, one by one, and describe to the students how we turn them into images to place them on the parts of the car. I do this by overlaying another transparency with the numbered words on top of the car transparency. (Once I've shown them a few examples, I ask for the students' help in creating the images to go with the words.)

When we've covered all twenty words, I make sure again that the students understand what we're doing. We quickly review the car and its contents one more time. I then remove the sheet with the words, and ask my students to write down all the words they can remember. (I leave the transparency with the car and numbered loci on the screen, since they haven't had time to master all the loci yet.)

The results vary, but not very much. With group after group, more than half of the students recall all twenty words at the end of this demonstration. They are usually rather pleased with themselves and with the method of loci at this point, so I then reveal to them that the concrete images we memorized were really mnemonic keywords for concepts from the lecture, and that many could appear on the next exam.

I'll illustrate with one of the sets of words I have used. (And I think you too will recognize most of the psychological terms, if you've been reading the Memory Master Tips and Facts.)

Words I Gave My Students	**Psychological Terms They Represent**
Cash register	Sensory register[5]
Shortstop	Short-term memory
The Terminator	Long-term memory
Code ring	Encoding
Grocery store	Storage
Golden retriever	Retrieval
Phone call	Recall
Ignition	Recognition
Hearse	Rehearsal
Organ	Organization

[5] A very brief, automatic visual or auditory memory store that precedes short-term memory.

Laboratory	Elaboration[6]
Al	Verbal elaboration
Image	Imagery elaboration
Key	Keyword method
Locust	Method of loci
Metal men	Metamemory
Prison	Personal variables
Tusk	Task variables
Stradivarius violin	Strategy variables
Fish in the sea	Deficiencies (production or mediation)[7]

Let's jump now from my college classroom into your own home. If you're homeschooling your children, you could adapt this demonstration for use with your own young charges. Depending on their ages, you could use a ten- or twelve-word list to begin with (using concrete words such as *chair* and *dog*). Instead of one complex figure, you could use a series of figures (as I've done in question 15). You needn't use transparencies; plain old paper will do. Show your children a set of loci from this mnemonic house. Use the foyer if ten is enough. If you want to demonstrate with more, throw in other rooms or substitute the study, which already has twenty locations.

As for the words, adapt them to a subject you've recently been teaching your children about. I've done this in my classes with

[6] Memory strategies that are based on elaborating or adding to the material to be remembered, either verbally, such as creating a story, or through imagery, as we've done throughout this book.

[7] Mediation deficiency refers to the inability to use a strategy. Infants and individuals with dementia have a mediation deficiency for these mnemonics. Production deficiency refers to the failure to use a strategy even though the capacity is there. Most people are production deficient in mnemonics. They don't use them because nobody ever taught them about mnemonics!

subject matter from the biology of puberty: a pit represented the pituitary gland, an adding machine represented the adrenal gland, and so on. Adapt these techniques for your children and their school subjects, and you'll help foster a new generation of artists and masters (artists in the art of memory and masters of their course's subject matter!) You'll add another unique benefit to those that homeschooling already affords.

MEMORY MASTER TIPS AND FACTS

QUESTION 29

Do artificial memory systems replace traditional methods of study?

By no means. Artificial memory systems merely supplement and enhance tried-and-true methods of study. They're additional arrows in our quivers of learning techniques. We should employ *metamemory* to determine when they're needed and when they're not. In this book we use them all the time, because we're learning *how* to use them. In real learning situations, we need not load our crossbows with massive iron bolts when a spongy little Nerf arrow will hit the target.

Conclusion

From Memory and Understanding to Faith and Works

"Faith apart from works is barren."

James 2:20

"To be well-versed in Scripture and all the sayings of the philosophers will not profit you if you are without God's love and his grace."

Thomas à Kempis, *Imitation of Christ*

"My brothers and sisters, let us be wary of praying to Christ with our mouths, but remaining mute in our life."

St. Augustine, in Thomas Hand's *Augustine on Prayer*

"Contemplata aliis tradere" ("To pass on to others the fruits of contemplation")

Motto of the Dominican Order: Translation from Gerald Vann's *The Aquinas Prescription*

The blueprints for our mnemonic house of faith, our "Christianized artificial memory," are now laid out. I hope that a great deal of construction is also complete. But even when this house is finished, we must recall that our Father's realm has many mansions. There still is so much more we could commit to memory: thousands of biblical passages, biblical chronology and personages, facts about the organization of the liturgical calendar, the structure of the Mass, important creeds and prayers. I leave it to you to determine which additions you might like to add to your mnemonic house of faith.

The mnemonics we explored — the use of mental imagery in general, the method of loci, the keyword method, and the number/word conversion system — are but mental or cognitive tools. Build with them what you may, and build at the pace and in the manner that suits you. If you've learned the house of this book, please feel at home and use it to your benefit. If you've become adept and wish to expand your mnemonic real estate, imagine additional rooms added on. Perhaps better still, *create mnemonic rooms from your own house and church*. When it comes to locations, the familiar best helps us capture and hold on to the new.

Mnemonic systems first work *externally*; that is, you'll need the actual pictures of these rooms to assist you until they've been committed to memory. Early on, you might find yourself stuck on, let's say, the last of the capital sins, but a quick glance at that living-room doorway into the dining room will trigger that picture of the giant *sloth* blocking your path. When you've really mastered the locations, you won't need to refer to the picture, because you'll have represented them *internally*, in your own head.

We also used some rooms up to three or four times. With practice, you'll find that the different sequences will hang together. You'll imagine the sloth in the doorway when going through the capital sins. When you reach that point in the books of the Old Testament, you'll have that sloth again, this time biting your toe, so *Tobit* will come to mind. If you're reciting the books of the New Testament, this same spot will call to mind a Titan, reminding us of the book of *Titus*, and the books recalled in sequence before it will bring the Titan, not the sloth, to mind, for you'll have recalled another Greek giant, the Colossus of Rhodes, a few locations back to remember the letter to the *Colossians*. Also, because of their orderly arrangement, if you're stuck, you'll often recall what you're looking for by recalling any terms from the same room and then working backward or forward to your desired location.

Oh yes. I almost forgot. What about retention of this material over time? If we don't use our muscles, they gradually atrophy. The same applies to information we've memorized, even with such mnemonics. To be truly mastered, they must be refreshed and repeated now and again. If you'll recall, this necessity of repetition was included as step four in St. Thomas's own description of artificial memory.

But did you know that even muscles have "memory"? If allowed to atrophy through disuse, a muscle once built up will grow back more quickly than before, if again submitted to the proper exercise. So too with these mnemonics. If you master some set of this material and let it fade over time, when you come back to it again, you'll settle right back in to the rooms and soon possess again all of their contents.

There, essentially, is the "memory" part of this chapter's title. My expert role in this book, of course, has concerned the mnemonics (and I express thanks to religious and scholarly readers for bearing with this amateur's attempts to apply a little theological gloss here and there). Memory is but the first step, although a very important step, in the virtue of prudence, and the pinnacle of prudence is living wisely in accordance with the right reason of the Christian faith.

On now to understanding. Our mnemonic goal exceeds rote memory alone. We seek not to repeat these facts of the Faith like a parrot, but to *understand* them like a "*rational* animal" made in God's image. That is why I have endeavored (I hope not *too* tediously or pedantically) to provide some highlights and guide you to sources in the Bible, the *Catechism*, the *Summa*, and elsewhere, so these subjects can be pursued in depth for real richness of understanding. But even here, the value of memory should not be underestimated.

Memory does not oppose understanding. We need them both. We can't carry the *Summa* around in our pockets, let alone the Bible and two thousand years of the writings of the Church. But we can carry around in our heads as much of this vital information that we take the trouble to commit to memory. Then, even when we don't have access to those books, we'll still be able to meditate upon the information we've memorized. This is a real advantage. Wouldn't it be hard to chew something that kept slipping out of your mouth? So too is it hard mentally to "chew on" things we can't remember.

"To Faith and Works" reads the last part of this last chapter's title, and this is really the most important part, for it relates to the true "end" of this book. Why bother to "memorize the Faith"? So that we may better *practice* and *live* the Faith. The letter of St. James is among my favorite epistles, because it so clearly makes the case that the Christian life is not only a matter of *belief*, but also a matter of *practice* informed and inspired by that belief. "You believe that God is one" states James, "you do well. Even the demons believe — and shudder" (2:19). Soon after comes that breathtaking line, "faith apart from works is barren" (or "faith without works is dead" in some translations). After all, what did St. Paul tell us and St. Thomas Aquinas so carefully explain? Charity is the greatest of virtues, and charity works.

Let's consider the quotation from St. Augustine about praying with one's mouth, but remaining mute with one's life. Do we show the integrity to practice what we preach? To put this in modern lingo, do we "walk our talk"? Now, talking or preaching is, of course, quite important. St. Augustine and St. Thomas Aquinas, not to mention Christ himself, did much invaluable preaching.

But those two saintly men, and that one holy God-Man, clearly also lived what they preached. These mnemonics can certainly serve as an aid to speaking or preaching, but we must also seek to keep our mouths and our hearts in the same place.

Next, to Thomas à Kempis, the fifteenth-century monk. Have you read his simple, yet astounding *Imitation of Christ*, for centuries the spiritual bestseller second only to the Bible? Please look at the quotation one more time. Studying the sayings of the Scriptures and philosophers we have done aplenty. But we must take care not to get frozen in their words alone. They should rather light a fire in us that drives us to put their wise counsel to practice in Christian charity.

Last but not least, let's look at the motto of the Dominicans, the order chosen by St. Thomas Aquinas. This was a religious order of preachers and teachers, and St. Thomas realized early on that it was the right order to house the gift of intellect God had given him. Thomas built that intellect to unexcelled heights and expressed it prolifically. But all that contemplation was fired by charity. He did it to glorify God and to benefit man. His massive body of magnificent writings, and even those few little paragraphs on the importance of artificial memory, are the fruits of his contemplation. We can live on those fruits today, if I may borrow again from Pope John XXII, like the ancient Egyptians lived on the corn stored by Joseph.

There's so much good work to be done by those who would imitate Christ. As the son of a carpenter, Christ himself surely realized the value of good tools. The memory aids presented in this book are tools in our mental and spiritual tool belts. For most people, without a competent craftsman to guide them, these tools will remain sadly unknown and unused.

But we're among the fortunate ones, because the craftsman who crafted the *Summa Theologica* has shown us how to use them. Go to him now.

MEMORY MASTER TIPS AND FACTS

QUESTION 30

How can I make the most of this book in the years ahead?

I answer in the very words of St. Thomas Aquinas himself: *Memoria non solum a natura proficiscitur, sed etiam habet plurimum artis et industriae* (*ST*, II-II, 49, 1): "Memory not only arises from nature, but is also aided by art and diligence." So return to this book again and again, and practice with diligence the art of memory!

Afterword

An Ode to Memorization

MEMORY NOW NOT FORGOTTEN

Memory now not forgotten,
Power of Mind so generous,
Words once mouthed by the Begotten,
In your vaults you hold for us.
Your stores shall not be sparse or rotten,
Now your Name rings true to us.

Given to us by the Father,
Glorified by his own Son,
Some of us say, "Oh, why bother?
My school days are long past gone.
Give me Understanding rather,
Deep Meaning to chew upon."

How think thoughts you can't remember?
How chew food your mouth can't hold?
Memory's not Mind's least member,
Restore now Her throne of old.
Through Memory do we recall
The good words God's prophets told.

Memorize the Faith!

Stone rejected by the builders,
Now you are the Cornerstone.
Your job is not to bewilder,
You mark our minds with what's His own.
Entrance you charge not a guilder,
Making your Mansions our own.

Build upon Imagination,
Art of Memory, gifts bestow.
Part of Prudence's creation,
Guiding good lives here below.
Helpful guide to meditation,
Holding for us what we know.

You have shown us strange mnemonics.
You let St. Thomas guide our way.
Angelic, and not demonic,
Is this new pow'r we learned today.
And was it not a bit ironic,
Forgetting Memory, anyway?

The End

Biographical Note

Kevin Vost

Kevin Vost (b. 1961) has taught psychology for the University of Illinois at Springfield, MacMurray College, and Lincoln Land Community College. He serves as a Research Review Committee Member for American Mensa, a society promoting the scientific study of human intelligence.

An Invitation

Reader, the book that you hold in your hands was published by Sophia Institute Press.

Sophia Institute seeks to restore man's knowledge of eternal truth, including man's knowledge of his own nature, his relation to other persons, and his relation to God.

Our press fulfills this mission by offering translations, reprints, and new publications. We offer scholarly as well as popular publications; there are works of fiction along with books that draw from all the arts and sciences of our civilization. These books afford readers a rich source of the enduring wisdom of mankind.

Sophia Institute Press is the publishing arm of the Thomas More College of Liberal Arts and Holy Spirit College. Both colleges are dedicated to providing university-level education in the Western tradition under the guiding light of Catholic teaching.

If you know a young person who might be interested in the ideas found in this book, share it. If you know a young person seeking a college that takes seriously the adventure of learning and the quest for truth, bring our institutions to his attention.

www.SophiaInstitute.com
www.ThomasMoreCollege.edu
www.HolySpiritCollege.org

SOPHIA INSTITUTE PRESS

THE PUBLISHING DIVISION OF